theVictory of sex &Metal

Copyright © 2015 by Barbara Mor

All rights reserved. No part of this book may be used or reproduced in any manner without written permission from the Publisher, except in the case of brief quotations that may appear in articles and reviews.

"A Meeting with Barbara Mor," by Edgar Garcia, appeared originally in the *Los Angeles Book Review* of April 19th, 2014, under the title "Barbara Mor's *The Blue Rental:* Rooms Outside Hollywood, Hell, USA." Reprinted by permission.

"24/7 AND YR DREAMS, A Conversation with Barbara Mor, by Adam Engel," originally appeared, in somewhat different form, in the online magazine *Dissident Voice*, on June 14, 2004: http://www.dissidentvoice.org/June04/Engel0614.htm

A portion of "the Victory of sex & Metal" appeared originally in *Sulfur 28*, Spring 1991, ed. Clayton Eshleman

Cover design by Jennifer Gonzalez-Blitz
Typesetting by Maria Petrova

Library of Congress Cataloguing-in-Publication Data
Mor, Barbara. *The Victory of Sex and Metal*

ISBN: 978-0-9883343-4-2
Library of Congress Control Number: 2015909445

The Oliver Arts & Open Press
2578 Broadway, Suite #102
New York, NY 10025
http://www.oliveropenpress.com

theVictory of sex &Metal

/a retro metaphysical punk graffix from 1981/

THE OLIVER ARTS & OPEN PRESS

to K. A.
in awe & grief

Contents

About Barbara Mor	9
Foreword: "Mor: An Introduction" by Edgar Garcia	11
"the Victory of sex &Metal" by Barbara Mor	21
Afterword: "24/7 and Yr Dreams, A Conversation with Barbara Mor" by Adam Engel	63
Appendix: "An Email Exchange"	89
Appendix II: "A Note on Writing Seriously Today" by Barbara Mor	105

About Barbara Mor

Barbara Mor was born October 3, 1936, in San Diego, California. Her mother died when Mor was twelve. Mor lived with her father and stepmother, leaving home immediately after high-school. Attracted by the Beat Movement of the late 50s and early 60s, she lived and wrote in the Santa Cruz Mountains, Baja California, and Los Angeles before returning to San Diego to attend San Diego State University. In the late 60s Mor became involved with the Feminist Movement in San Diego. She taught poetry, gave readings and lectures, and helped compile local, limited-run poetry anthologies. Mor spent the mid-1970s in Taos, New Mexico, before moving to Albuquerque in 1979. During this period she published *Bitter Root Rituals* (WomanSpirit, 1975), *Mother Tongue* (Athena Press, 1977), and *Winter Ditch* (Second Porcupine Press, 1982), and began work on *The Great Cosmic Mother* (Harper & Row, 1987), widely considered among the great American feminist texts of the 20th century. Mor moved to Portland, Oregon, in the late 1990s, drawing on her experience in the Southwest to forge a prose style that is as innovative and demanding as it is compelling. *The Blue Rental,* a collection of these prose texts, was published by The Oliver Arts & Open Press in 2011. *The Victory of Sex and Metal* (The Oliver Arts & Open Press, 2015), completed during the Spring of 2014, marked Mor's return to poetry and her stark vision of the American Southwest.

Barbara Mor died on January 24, 2015. She is survived by her three children — Caleb, Joanna, and Rhen.

Mor: An Introduction

by Edgar Garcia

"Isn't the true poet or painter a seer? Isn't [s]he, actually, the only seer we have on earth?"

—J.D. Salinger, "Seymour: An Introduction"

I

"IT'S IMPORTANT TO ME that you write," James Dean said to 19-year old Barbara Mor when he dropped her off at her boardinghouse on Franklin and Beachwood. They had dined at the famous Villa Capri on McCadden Place, where Mor remembers Dean "referenced that Frenchman's poem & then recited barbare... barbare... barbare... just that word three times." Rimbaud's poem describes the bleeding flesh and the fires that underlie the fanfare of heroism and mythology. It was a prescient poem to invoke. Six days later Dean was killed in an auto accident on his way to Salinas, giving rise to one of Hollywood's greatest myths, and Mor was left at the beginning of a life disarticulating the "nauseous allegories" of America, picking apart the bleeding flesh and conflagrations that underlie our national fanfare.

Some know Mor as the co-author of *The Great Cosmic Mother*, a tome on Goddess worship published in 1987. But her life's work as a poet taking apart the visceral reality beneath our national mythology appeared in Clayton Eshleman's *Sulfur*, the influential literary magazine of the 1980s and 1990s. This was a brutal time for Mor. She was living in poverty, often homeless, on the streets of Tucson and Albuquerque, in total eclipse with an abusive partner, "a pharmacopeia, he was; junkie, street thug, Mexican boxer, pimp prostitute hitman [...] a notorious crazy street person." She saved what she could from the slow fire eating her skin, "sitting in 24/7 BurgerKing with free coffee refills into infinity, air conditioning, writing in notebooks." Into these notebooks she put the thoughts and words that became the material of her first book of poems in more than thirty years, *The Blue Rental*, the evisceration recently published by Eric Larsen and Adam Engel's Oliver Arts & Open Press.

The Blue Rental displays the gangrenous nerve and bone of life on the streets of the American southwest. Alternating in focus from cosmology to autobiography and politics, the book of poems in prose spans eons but never loses sight of "the Soul w/out a Home in America." Informed by a deep curiosity and sensitivity, *The Blue Rental* touches on a wide range of topics like homelessness, Neanderthals, nuclear proliferation, the shape of native time, the spiritual cost of American consumerism, and the Juárez Murders (the ongoing spree of women-killing in Ciudad Juárez which Mor considers "the Guernica of our Time"), to name only a few. But its greatest triumph is to bring these far-reaching meditations into a single epiphanic study of the spiritual state of America today, a bright moment in the light of a raging and all-consuming fire. The opening section of the poem welcomes us to its elusive place, a crime scene like a flame in blueshift:

    blue womb or rental room of empty houses inside a vast night
    blue adobes along a street are radiant with such light   strangely
    occupied as museum or uterus blue immense of a universe
    looped and rerun perpetual for the stars insomnia   who never
    sleep   it cant get born out of in which it always dwells
                        or who lives in the other rooms
    who knows why they continue to love it watching static when
    the show is over   or now stare at a blue screen   *a hypnotic*
    stare injects blue into everything   1 light year is 6trillion miles
    so they do not sleep or dream   trance is a slower brain as
    gods watch an indifferent spectacle
    Devonian 395-345million yearsbce   swamps forests ferns
    something crawls from sea to wet green then fish may walk
    4limbed vertebral land dwellers 360millionyearsbce   repeat
    250million dinosaurs 65million mammals 8million hominids
    humans 200,000 years   *from explosions of Cambrian*
    multicells Great Ordovician biodiversification   *methane*
    ammonia hydrogen+lightning spark=amino acids 3.5billion
    years   *a universe they say*   *13.75 billion years*   *began*
    that eyes stare at such distance   or the crime it means
            what is a chronic absence to do with enormous pain
    to create an Other to end the Solitude of Everything that IS
    it gropes blind first invention of feelers eyes beauty words
    i look up at starry mirrors and desire translation into words
    and becomes what it has become   i am therefore i am
    i am not obscure   *i do not remember the crime*

In a way, Mor's view of the US in the 20th century was paradigmatic. She was born in 1936 in California "before the freeway, before plastic & fastfood franchises," and watched it transform with war industry and suburban sprawl. As a teenager eager to escape an oppressive home life, she was a beach bum and later a beatnik in the Hollywood area. At age 17, she married "a guy from Las Vegas" and by the end of the decade she was living "in Baja with a Beat artist." When the 1960s reared its head with the assassination of JFK, she was a first-year student at San Diego State University (then known as San Diego State College), where she stayed for six years until she walked out nine units shy of a degree "cuz in WorkStudy Id found obscure books on ancient matriarchies in Mega/Neolithic Europe & the Mediterranean buried in the basement, & after all my education (including Anthro, Comparative Religion, World Lit & Mythology etc etc) Id never been introduced to such texts."

She then began to write for a San Diego women's newspaper, *Goodbye To All That*, a series of essays that would form the basis of her work in *Great Cosmic Mother*. Amid the political explosions occurring on college campuses, Mor became more deeply involved in the women's liberation movement, editing an international all-women poetry anthology, until the paranoia programmatically disseminated by CoIntelPro leaked into the movement, causing a crippling "politics of serious infighting." She left just as Ronald Reagan's governorship put the squeeze on welfare mothers, dispossessing California of one of its greatest minds. She moved to New Mexico. In 1987, she moved again to Tucson, believing the prestige of recently published *Great Cosmic Mother* might secure her a lectureship at the University of Arizona (hoping to simultaneously write a comparative study of Celtic and Mesoamerican spiritual systems). Instead, she failed to get even cleaning work in their maintenance department. She was soon on the streets. Mor remembers a particularly telling episode during this period of homelessness when she was caught sponge-bathing in a bathroom at the University. She was run out by a maintenance worker even as her book was being taught at the University. The University, she says, "was not home to my body even though its Library might house my book."

But the same alienation from the academy kept Mor in close contact with a life and world unimaginable to many. *The Blue Rental* is a collection inhabited by the frayed people, spirits, and animals she met in those Tucson years: homeless children, roaches, scorpions, Maya sorcerers, women beaters, heroin addicts, wild dogs, prostitutes, rapists, and murderers. With a Rimbaud-like eye to the conflagration beneath the epic fanfare, Mor's book shows us the grim scene beneath the surface myth of American life. And the deeper she goes the more textually distorted the book gets. In one of the poems, "Linguistic Duplex," the poet cuts textually into the future when she sits to read a women's magazine with a homeless girl while the girl appears in a news report about her own murder. The girl is snatched away by her perplexed mother in an interplay of time, text, and terror that recalls scenes from the novels of William Burroughs and the films of David Lynch. (A portion of this poem can be heard read by the poet in a recording that is available online.)[1] Each page turns into hell, whose heat keeps its denizens from sleeping, lying awake worrying if exit is possible. Mor's basic conviction is that it is. But it is unclear what labor, belief, or supernatural power is required for it. "Tricky angels and canny demons" abound:

> the girl does not know if he sees or truly
> lives in darkness, wearing dark glasses at midnight the burn
> retinas of his partner sometimes spin like tornadoes they
> share between them one white stick w/ruby knob. Poco
> thin in jeans white t-shirt Loco even skinnier sometimes a
> baseball cap looking backward. they ate everything, everything
> one dish after another back to the table never sated never fat
> they ate all night. clowns to nightworkers, a rapid
> turnover
> Those old people fed the Sun
> corazones humanos, wrapt in warm tortilla flesh
> ancient Mesoamerican fastfood: burritos por El Dios
> a brown thumb jerks at the outside mirage, 4am parkinglot
> crouched before dawn neon smog pulsed in blackbeats of unslept
> cars. Gringos feed god farts. Talk about a religion
> Tonan, Our Mother, w/many wiry dirty fingers he taps the
> table, they could be spiderlegs. what does She eat? Creature
> excrement menstrual blood raw placentas corpses. dump
> all this good food in the toilet, guero. rivers oceans it becomes
> water. Pocho stares into his Coke. I think Im drinking it
> no wonder She croaks
> the girls body appears at the table, he leans & deeply
> sniffs her crotch. no sangre de las flores, relojes de la luna
> no iron no sulfur no ammonia no chemistry between you
> pero bugspray, no morbid bodies! his fingers on in & out of her
> in strange ways, the starving maggots. organs lockt in cans cars
> antidecomposition boxes, UR coffins. Ocho very excited now
> digs Bic from levi pocket clicks openLight flares upward thru

---

[1] https://soundcloud.com/lareviewofbooks/barbara-mor-reading-the-blue-rental?utm_source=Newsletter+September+2014&utm_campaign=Oliver+Reaches+Readers&utm_medium=email

his skull becomes an owl reverse ocelot, fountain of Death.
the girl stares & smiles. this dialog between them quantum
tlachtli faster than light she like many others mildly retarded
yet cheerful therefore. from the top of his head come fireworks,
Nuclear explosion
my girlfriend the Witch ate my heart w/her eyes or just looking
she can chew off yr leg muscle, no pain, you just fall over. is
that nice?
no counting for Taste
speaking of waist, la cinga, news item Aug 02: the Equator
circumference is growing. The world is fat
eats too much junk
speaking of justice, his finger sibylically moves upon the
air, Bovine Spongiform Encephalopathy, a chronic wasting disease.
todo el mundo is wasted. I have dumps in my head of dead
species, upsidedown extinct little toenails & babyeyes. maybe it is
these cannibals, his fingers fluttering many unseen knives fly out
embed surrounding neurons of eaters. Bovas Sponges Encephalants,
mis hijos! revenge of bushmeat
after all it is not brain surgery
do you believe in poetry?
a mute exchange of stares thru black mirrors, the smoke
curling up from somewhere they have no cigarettes, then
Chuyo y Puyo laugh it is a very dry laughter like snake
rattles behind a rock in the arroyo
In 1536 Cabeza de Vaca y 3 companeros crawl delirious from
this desert back in Sinaloa bullshit their homey slavers re
7 cities of gold I saw them in El Norte
1540 Coronado goes after the gold of Cibola
Mr Head of a Cow Senor Cowhead who hallucinates civilization
from a shitpile
Cibola is a softdrink i think

No longer sipping Cibola, since the late 1990s Mor has lived in Portland, Oregon. Her recent writings have left behind the Tucson experiences, turning instead toward the "shavd polymorphd" world after September 11, 2001. Inhabited by terrorists, quantum ghosts, (dis-) honest politicians, and other things which may or may not exist, this world—in which she sees Joan of Arc argue with Dostoyevsky and Pussy Riot play in a clitoral-shaped cosmos—is "not doomed," Mor stresses, "by Nature but by DumbIdeas." Her life's work has been an untangling on this basic premise, giving a corpus and destiny to Dean's insight that it was important that she should write and in her writing reveal the bleeding flesh and conflagration beneath our American fanfare. Some of these writings—poetic and polemical—are available at her blog. Her next collection, a trilogy titled Metals, is currently unsmelting itself at her computer in paradise.[2]

II

I met Barbara this winter. Trekking to Portland on Interstate 5, I felt myself mainlining a 1,300-mile artery parallel to the Pacific Ocean, winding inland to British Columbia on the 99 and traversing the peninsula of Baja California on the 1. When I approached the Columbia River, I thought of Smohalla, the 19th-century Wanapum who brought back the Dreamer faith and the Washat dance in order to resist colonial incursion of the area. He told the white settlers that he would not cut into the breast of his mother to farm and profit. Instead, he would be fed by her as he had always been — with respect and admiration for regenerative cosmic processes.

> You ask me to cut grass and make hay and sell it, and be rich like white men! But how dare I cut off my mother's hair? It is a bad law, and my people cannot obey it. I want my people to stay with me here. All the dead men will come to life again. Their spirits will come to their bodies again. We must wait here in the homes of our fathers and be ready to meet them in the bosom of our mother.

Today Smohalla's beloved valleys make most of the hazelnuts, Christmas trees, and grass seed sold in North America. I am told that a sizable number of the people that work these plots are undocumented, indigenous migrants from Mexico, many of whom speak neither English nor Spanish. The time, texture, and terror of history enfold: In preparation to revitalize the Dreamer faith and Washat dance, Smohalla walked in agony southward through what he called the "Land of the Dead": California, Mexico, New Mexico, Arizona, and Utah, over paths perhaps walked by the Mixtec and Nahua workers of these fields, over paths perhaps walked by Barbara Mor.

She welcomed me to her small, book-filled apartment with a cup of tea, apologizing that she had no snack to offer since, having overrun the bookshelves, her books had taken over the cupboards too. A drowsy cat sat in a patch of sunlight. Barbara and I sat across from each other amid all the books, gradually becoming familiar with each other's physical presence after

---

[2] This essay was written in the spring of 2014, nine months before Mor's death, in January of 2015. The work referred to is published, as "The Victory of sex & Metal," in the pages of the book you are now reading.

nearly a year of email correspondence. We started by recapping how we had met. She had had her daughter contact me after finding that I posted some of her *Sulfur* writings to my blog. I had been taken by the flagrant intensity of her writing, riveted by its polemical propulsion heading God-knows-where:

> Life on Tuscon streets with an Aztec-Mayan streetfighter will of course Intensify It. It is a matter of enormously condensed and suspended energy, can blow up Universe with any microflick of the tail. But: is wholly unliterary, unhistoric. These exist still packed in DNA; as Pancho says, "I am the Book." No-word dream-state of images, magnetic fields, and body action. It needs a good translator. The energy of verbal work, writing, is a high-speed or short-wave radiation. My brain works, but it is long waves, below the sound-threshold. I mean I dont hear much going on in there: the metallic drone of the Malabar caves, one-way traffic on Lead St...

When I got her daughter's message, I thought that I was in trouble for posting the poems without permission. But I wasn't; the poet was happy to find herself found. I told her that I first came across her name as the author of *The Great Cosmic Mother*, to which she winced, disavowing the book, cursing the publishers, and condemning its title (which suggested that women could only be cosmic if they were mothers; she wanted to call it "The First God"). I told her that I had learned a great deal from the book and that I had found it provocative and inspiring. She admitted that it had some good to it.

Dedicated to her mother and Meridel LeSueur, the book begins with a prayer from the Takic-speaking Indians of Southern California entirely of a piece with Smohalla's regenerative cosmic vision: "As the moon dieth and cometh to life again/so we also having to die, will live again." The book tells the story of the programmatic destruction of matrifocal paganism and the socialist political structures with which it is associated. But, in addition to a deep history of women, paganism, and communalism, the book is also a kind of *Woman's Technicians of the Sacred*, rich with poetry, spiritual writings, and traditions collected from around the world. These stories, incantations, artifacts, technologies, and strategies are the counterprogram to the erasure, silence, and destruction. They are the texts by which the moon is supposed to live again.

As it turns out, I am visiting when the moon is in Scorpio. The scorpion is a creature that controls its destiny. It prefers the sting of its own tail to the assault of an enemy ("can blow up Universe with any microflick of the tail"). Curled into a crescent, its tail is said to regenerate, maybe because it looks like a crescent moon. Barbara and I talk about destiny. She tells me that she always knew she was a writer ("at age 8 Id declared myself a writer and I think the universe heard me; from then on everything was part of the required course"). Still, there was a hellhound on her heels from the start. Her mother, who played pop songs on piano and taught Barbara to read music and play ("my first poetry was Gershwin, Lorenz Hart, and Cole Porter"), died when she was 12. She married at 18 to escape her father and "evil" stepmother's home, didn't find the experience of marriage "educative enough," so fled to Hollywood to meet Dean. She hangs out with him a few times in the week before his death at the crossroads, another hellhound, "last minute he decided to drive the car, thus [...] destiny." In the years that follow she stays in Hollywood, taken by the growing Beat scene.

> Low rent, minimum wage jobs easy to get and leave and get another one, 10 books a week from downtown LA library plus Pickwick Bookstore where Zen and Existential and Beat books were shelved. I lived on coffee, cigarettes, green apples, cans of jack mackerel, and lots of Spearmint gum. And books.

She adds that every night she walked from Highland east to Hollywood and Vine to hang out at an outside coffee bar at Hollywood Ranch Market and talk with other weird people. She asks if I'd ever heard of the 24-hour Hollywood Ranch Market. I hadn't; it closed a decade before my family moved around the corner from Santa Monica and Hudson. My memories of growing up in the Hollywood area are of vatos, punks, and transgender prostitutes. Not beatniks. We talk about how much LA changed in the last century and how much it is changing today. LA and the Island of California; Aztlán, apocalypse, and Atlantis; terraformation missions gone haywire. When Orion got to Crete he hunted with Artemis and Leto and boasted that he would kill every beast of the island. Gaia heard this and freaked. To stop him she sent a scorpion to sting Orion to death. Thus... destiny. Orion was elevated as a warning in the sky; to the rest of the hemisphere it is a constellation that hangs over Southern California.

Evening overtakes the sparsely furnished room in which we are sitting across from each other. We stare like moons at their own reflection in a darkening river. Barbara's sharp blue eyes shine over her face etched like pale sandstone. Conversation with her is aeolian and eonic; talk of geological processes, Neanderthals, and ancient ceremonial magic are carried as if by gusts to discussions of Charles Fort, Aleister Crowley, Gertrude Stein, and quantum poetics ("Quantum Mechanics seems to describe a Poetic Field to me"). Intellectual, aesthetic, political, mystical, and cultural activities are fused in this field in an intelligent, exciting way. Her voice is hoarse from so much speaking. Feeling intensely moved by our day together, I ask her if she could throw me a spread of *The Book of*

Thoth, her preferred Tarot deck for various reasons. With a wary but sly smile she tells me that she hasn't thrown in many years — but that she will on this occasion. She walks to one of the bookshelves and pulls down a large, dusty box that opens to a deck with worn edges and surfaces faded from long use. She has me cut the deck in three deliberate steps, takes it up with her staggering, shining, sandstone hands, and begins to drop the cards as we nosedive into quantum fields.

Edgar Garcia received his doctorate in American literature from Yale University in 2015. He teaches at the University of Chicago.

theVictory
of sex
&Metal

this is a different planet Knife Boy

not born from this   i dont think   from a cunt built
on earth   where does light needle yr skin some ice
ink seeks a cruel expression   this was poetry
long ago   or long ago a mental cauldron of first
explosions experiments on fire invented bitch elements
some acids a night excretes and they dissolve yr face
gears guts fists clenchd in a direction   like Fate
huge stiletto teeth grind down and spit me out
                                                                  or maybe not
where do you think
maybe it was dead as a future
i dont think   a machine proceeds moves forward   it
doesnt think   it is a function   glass silica skin crushd
red of acute mirror intersections   they hurt each other
beautifully   sexual metal   if this is me
they hurt each other in the meaning   of a world
                                                  orient me
among the metalloids *float body pieces* worms
and flowers soft interiors do not exist do not rot
except stench of dead resisters   abattoir dumpsters
flesh otherwise ornament   worn naked   as a ghost
a garden postbiologic even in alleys pissd by plasm
rats   i surrender thought sentiments of slow
motion suicide   wearing a torn heart remnant of
brutal fashion   street eyes air walls of appendages
constructed to work   evisceration works
i was sleeping   i/you dreamd it
     sleep or dreams not yet invented   or time extractd
i dont think clock hallucinations spermd of earth
what do you know
brainspasm of flesh scrapd by huge planets of steel
metalfold hairy w/ needles in yr throat   i dont belong
sensd lost here   who belongs   i belong
at the End   beautifully
as if needing me   this disaster makes me
like a mother

Mechanical Girl speaks

2

war   flesh wars with ulterior night and loses   this is history

a fact of something victorious   *as apocalyptic beasts sleek
in their luminous metals emergd from Earth*   these are the
words   how it feels in a brain when wheels roll over   giants
speak   and matter is expressd   ores thick mud excreta blood
interior language   into a history of   Body is there to be used
therefore   as Time manufacturd of a wound
                                          it is glorious
and the parade of vehicles triumphant   the great machinery
revolves as axials epochs of grinding of gears of oceans as
gods open their mouths   so many screaming vulvas open
into mythic worlds   a roar of deep caverns doors as orifices
to be plunderd or orate a final sound of nothing   this is
ragnarok that will be Death but unlike others   my world

women in particular the decorative sex   if human hair long
female hair drifts from their antennae like flags   or labia
spread open on chrome grills   a slick trophy   or confetti of
skin drifting down on us   as dust   we thought it flattery
as girls so manufacturd and cool we cannot think   cannot
speak   face in a mirror construct of oil   it cannot care   as
the ship naglfar compressd of dead metallic fingernails
once clawd guitars as erotic flesh   and riding the gorgeous
back of the sea   it takes her down
                                      memorys body *as
all the beasts convergd in catastrophic metals*   is a stuffd
mouth all knowledge shutup beaten down inside is hard
rock   absoluteTime   nothing speaks until earth speaks   or
mantic utters   spoils of war&warriors speak   their engines
of awful groins humming or purring or rumbling   and slow
haunches more beautiful than women   their animal eyes
seek nothing but are terrible lights   *some voluspa growl
or howl of extinct things*   or death orgasm that is not me

this is history   is history of my body

3

exstasis it begins
it was from extasis   LLatin – terror < ekstasis Greek
astonishment, distraction < existanai – to displace, derange;
ex (out of) histanai (to place)

to be place a lurid earth some ghostly dust whirling in
its own Time how long it takes when there is no Time
condense condensd clenchd as muscle does not yet exist
but shining glowing fire thru dust as desire to Be realizd
gruesome &alone it must become *metal* injectd hot as
veins manufacturing into pallid flesh thru skin/walls of
Unknown nerve like wire
i did this Solitary and voluptuous of my body what it is
a cold thing heatd up with purpose derangd what it is
means to Be when every surface is a cunt all matter
molten and Alive until it hardens is then a Being of rock
who remembers *i was* in alchemy of fire you do not
remember until me
   Lat metallum < Gk metallon – mine mineral metal
corporeal fusion mind who conducts heat and electricity
infuse a body this is thought
'One might almost say, her body thought' – John Donne
so from a brain or a uterus or a hand or bowel what is
a difference from the same desire power always in the
dark juice lava convulsions and blood darkness before
yr eyes i perform exstasies of excretion extraction
gestation billions of years hallucinant of colors rush
and moan of surrenderd bodies how many planets and
objects and thoughts orgasmd matter the deep dream of
darkness and Time
   we are using words as *earth vulva* as if it was alive
god is an erotic universe   deal w/it

* * * * * * * *

you were that shiny thing i invented Alone
   earth is an erotic animal and yr mind the material
   imagination as brilliant animal   as actual torc
   and torso which must be Thought or some poem
   incandescent i can believe it is hard to express
theOther
from conscious darkness forgd a dark inside 1st orgasms
then result as chromiums and pitch w/colors thick

interior jewels and fuel carbon violet yellow red chalk
water blood effusions as turnd in its own arms and
wanting more &more enormously appears surprisd
by invention acidic hot & distilled hours left to jut
&glisten this is poetry of the 1st thought as if all
originally desired &forgotten thus a terrible &fine
solution of same flesh beautifully fucking itself but
not the same tooth beautifully piercd itself but not
&the *negrido*   rot and rut sulfuric like classic night
stenchd w/jammd parts pitslime &perfume
                                                                  &all the blackness changd
iridescent blue &green this is poetry of the kill our
alchemical welding of earth to itself like a knife is
made it requires the same fire the same recognition
we are dangerous &strange   then we are Time&
are forgotten evolving conscious bodies mated &
gorgd our calciums as clastic bones and angles our
elements drenchd &heavy w/a Mental fire who does
not remember me before existence but multiplies the
bitter salt sweet poison of sensation multiplies
                                        2 warriors eruptiond of
1 solitude as originally defind we start out young as
total and clean   and mutual death we become w/out
knowing why   as all sweat shimmerd light of yr sole
weapon and all wombs night where this dream is
made you must separate out i must repeat 2 lovers
become a terrible army   Time becomes a religion
w/out me   2 warriors a noble pain neither and both
as i am a 1st same hunger beauty grief consumes
all Self or not
      lovd as a brilliant animal swallowd shit void
excretes exudes you swallows yr loss exchanges
for something else or some engines of mythic
flesh or biologic machinery i can do this Alone
earth was an erotic animal   comprehend this

                   * * * * * * * *

convergd us in all directions as shining vehicles
something you/i invent (comprehend) the
metaphysicals of it
               implacable as seas will be convulsd as
our 1st night never forget this as the passions extractd
before Time and before that fuel and before that and

before that an age of final thingsLast demonstrations a
design of something that will beDeath but all transformd
spectacularly   & we are earthclutchd into something
other it once was love it was said it was sad
'the unformed volcanic earth, a female thing' —RJeffers
if so it must be me takes yr eyes darkly inward down
or where in the dark machines from theDark engineerd of
theDark against its thought metal man metal animal
animal who shapes flesh into its suicide Time &orgasms
of matter before our eyes i performd   & would wish
our intersections over and over luxurious immolations or
material screams to recur as only heat lava rock eond
as exstasis of surrender repeats creation of anEarth
    yet made deep inside her lover/betrayer do w/this
what they do i can be thrown from tall bldgs a parade
of flowers extinctd plastoid dust or notorious ashes i
cannot believeMeans as once meant symbolically there
is no difference as advertisd or real the unutterd pain of
creatures a charade of images in the skull takes place
of dreams no longer powerful as machina glamorous&
cruel visions incorporate beyond us offer me as yrs
when you are anInvention   like all the others
the brain injectd w/shit the mind injectd w/fire all the
junkie arms of streets transfixd their slow acid motion
evolves as traffics in delirium my eyes injectd w/metals
trancd inks and flesh and bldgs into armies mindfully
born against us purposd beyond us hugely doom and
material pain as twistd w/mental motion over and over
rolld backwards into memory as stared thru sharp air
always stark and we are shadows
        thus sex gives up its fixt illusions   i can
fuck metal but should learn to love(it) if learn to die
unborn want pain unreal be only because you are yr all
surrounding bliss of hard objects into the heart cool
hard meltd hot it was said it was sad   w/you at theEnd
a weapon condensd from night explodes the night
i was an erotic thought   it died

4

                  turmoil what does that mean the usual night
im standing on a corner night the 1st darkness of a known
world   to survive [here] the necessity you are alone always
being alone the illusion of something crowds is only a
confusion between film/reality background running behind
yr body stark isolate of empty terrain one hunter one prey you
are (the last) body the final thought of the earth/world play
out/enact some long historical/dream that never finishd it
finishd them
the hunters are sundown traffic im blind continuous surf
on another planet overpowerd membranes huge vehicles
or interstellar traffic erase skin direction remembrance that
something was no one stops no one knows people on a raw
street they are residues of displacd time biosphere bad
luck suckd to a future Future landscape no one dreams can
stop we primitive remnants and then the hungers are out
now sundown in a real jungle they had some honor animals
respect animals beasts honor beasts man kills fear as dark
sport   something anything remains im standing
on a corner night my brains go off/on red/green the sign
change a language in the jungle of semiautomatics or the
final knife darkness enters everybodys eye yr motion and
Western civilization this huge armord vehicle armorous
vehicle of absolutist love or else but i hear you give
memories a deal i hear tongues memories a deal a dial
sweeps atmospheres time in everything
                                                make it real

   — ask me if i care
   — nobody

preponderance of history raw sludge break us down to
size the fact is in his black slouch leather jacket wearing
some other bodys dead skin always naked(never) only
alone costumd customd in solitude unacknowledgd
thus hes got need we say 4 love it is a lie he tells sells
yr face it always works the romantic moon of you the
un(i)(n)formd abyss he of all things sees in a mirror his
ulterior face but disembodied of yr encumbrance aroma
of yr story he likes the blood fresh from his cuts not yr
tidal dogchain dark fetid not his servitude thats only to
lean body leand on a night smoking he smokes in yr
eyes like stars are nebulae gas you could not breathe/
believe there but youd try to nothing nobody accumulatd

history he thinks his world is i know different but like
his dreamy version/dreamd diversion reality being my
repetition of all this then i forget
   — who cares
   — i disappear in cars

i think im wearing old levis brown baggy longsleevd
sweater no bra no cosmetics no jewelry after all it is hell
here im in hell   but prefer not do not identify
black guy jonesing for a fuck behind me at busstop here
the goddess Hel queen of his darkness [white/black] we
share her bones bony necessity to serve ubiquity sensate
time she wallows in blood he wants it suckd id drain
it all the red stuff unsanguind shadow disappears thus
down her magic throat otherwise fuckoff man fuck off
my skin crawls under masks and subterfuges refuges
in time we inhabit now in night essential to inhabit what
place findable alley garage cardboard box someones
dream sometimes beautiful or hit the CarlsJrBK allnite
booth 1 cup coffee eternal refills until dawn means it is
safe to close yr eyes somewhere park benches are 4 or
crosstown busrides for this 1 ride eternal refills when
drivers let it sometimes they want to talk flirt cute in
the moving emptiness sometimes they hate a whore
not open for bizness or drive into her as night splayd
out around their big machine
                             between aPoet aWhore a
mysticism of power oblique but final i can walk or
ride a pro who is invisible until the deal occurs,then
disappears   orTime ahead to kill the road ahead w/
no end a wasteland symbolically after all stripmall of
no return everybody needs to get off here before the
real the desert realEnd of the mind our consequence of
all juicd desperate time murders calld how we love it
toDeath surrounds you

                * * * * * * * *

  estrangd aspect in public mirror,only face i have left
Hel stationd of midnite lit CarlsJr bathroom peachpink
sulfurous aura of all things lonely alone selfcontemplatd
hangouts it is comforting tepid faucetwater hot coffee
eternal refills black no one exists the magicelectric blur
of rainbowlights beyond our glassy walls it is the desert

the gods return here a Bifrost bridge arcs outside over
CongressSt BurntHild inkd in mirrors why not any drunk
skull walking such streets everybody knows it ends in
night i see theOldGods over a shoulder hunchd under a
face(she)thinner saltd tan not bad not lovely not old not
ever young desirable as wise tough once now tired worn
everybody knew this always all fall down to be real
everyBody is fuckd here no distinction of qualities in
the glowerd dark
so the OldGods fell overboard Vikingships dreamd
shovd curious into the desert Pacific saltcrust the iced
blue eyes deepend centuries bottoms of oceans dark w/
estrangd mythologies   druggd here a vegetation of as
if all the water suckd off a planet what remains weird
unphotosynthd growths as radiant warts spikd poisond
lumps w/no eyes &their epic correspondents still not
dead halflife lowlife in their ultimate depths they are
gods yet drunk shrunk wizend lost as in timewreck as
wrackd w/hollow orbits too much seen not reconcild
hunchd in a sidebooth scruffy silent we are true gods
the parkd lot beyond caffeine night 2 vans ghosts in
their interiors deals are done powders of basalt lava
all the swimming squid sharks last flesh eatenMatterd
felld radiant bones fixt w/powers of desertd sagas
this is a(current)vision
               so i am Hel her attributes northern &
cold thought nothing like happiness is heroic deal w/it
volva of the street constant to be confusd w/netherly
female parts also apply dread of dead hallucinations
risen to walk miragd returnd of repressd as the iron
applies its heat to the muscles neurons mangld flat as
mirroragd thence gods shedded from skin alien in this
place w/our blued hands eyes as wheels spun fixedly
in some remote glacier derangd we invent engines lies
walk(w/purpose) or crawl infinitely returnd to sense
out of no mindsLand into this my attributes :Hel is a
woman
          i think therefor notes grown from a brain
write down allnite vigil centuried lines appear in face
skried for meaning as if blown sand blizzards of Time
stored in some witherd cave hellir a Matabrune tongue
her mouth open&open rimeclenchd at the end long
spasmd or pourd out dangerous once to be known 4am
bitter refills there is no doomMusic in their ears or

ginnungagap alarm the stolid woman keeps her head
down or stares thru them as desperation as the infinite
stare nothing is told keep distanceSilence wolf&snake
yr brothers lurkd another continent therefore visible in
yr face as they were crossd hot ironscars of their Iced
lips a simple brandname poetry ofExpression oral flare
in this yr singd dark my attributes Once tall thin tannd
leather our skins were bookcovers our interiors &yrs
read long ago recalld in delirium then burnt alive by
desertdSons my attributes :this ancient brain stared
at me in some synonymous mirror
        we have studied long now extinctd here we are
come   .the dark air is warm

            * * * * * * * * *

knifeBoy sits alone or is a lone the Holocene is over   [Bill McKibben]
someone sd now the EXocene the x-ing out of every
thing he can do that w/his eyes unseeing you
   if i say something deep
     — fuck you
in the vicinity of a world Love is not necessity only
poetry sd that or somebodys mother in the old days he
cant remember where he slept last nite
    — or nothing sez MechanicalGirl because it seems
alwaysNight the traffic proceeding thickens as milk
skim on acrid skin he drinks that way dawns caffeine
Enlightenment is tricky some passd soundsystem sez
this she is always talking to herself as another person
to another person is he imagind our planet imaginary
to our sense an invisible playmate of aSolitude this
has been considerd(con-sidereal :w/the stars) a long
nite is passd this way but KnifeBoys body against her
solid skin now&then or something out ofNothing is
also a birth of stars
                  how he lives dont ask nothing
is pretty here we inhabit bodies of whores &hustlers
or the rats feral jaws w/salvagd flesh pieces *winners*
those who deal whatLife dealt in their time&now rule
junk returnd to markets of theirKind(or batteries or
matches of thickbelts canndheat a rare ring intact w/
its swollen finger corpsewallets Eyeballs of a dead
loser a spoon to eat food that isnt there) a squalid
existence some wd say(in another century,they didnt

feel or see) we are immortal yet suffer paradox of
hunger forever also
                              KnifeBoy faces east the light
solid as a wall ofHeat nothing can climb out of it
climbs up his cool facade   born here or drifters the
clever sleep thru this place w/eyes unclosd abandond
store windows nothing looks in Nobody looks out
,& thru you /a city a construction a rock sweats its
minerals &angles of purposes toward whatEnd any
gestalt of a planets terminal autophagous swoon
    — hey KnifeBoy sez Shut up
    — its on the menu
                              &now there is a sweat
like grit filmd w/oil and how even gods will fill up
of strength of moisture and it is not beyond us but
inside us some ontologic sweat   outside in the street
rattlers of engines and their omnivorous wheels they
can unhinge their jaws to devour everything   as
Fenrir &her yawning gap long familiar or forgotten
in the ice,nobody hears this music in a desert will
appear asRevelations ,gunnd motors we employ a
silence tooHard to speak deafness of gears a crew of
terminators w/out appetite they will eat us we recall
them in old movies this is the caffeinesweat of gods
they run like flutterdfilm thru our eyes as they feastd
once in greatHalls some tossd bones in a dumpsite are
their names nothing utters   and they still act &they
still hunger in their gross machinery they outstrip
the movie why am i concernd it wonders as agony
inevitable a recycling of myth or minerals food&drink
of the same gods (we are)   &they cannot eat w/out
ghosts of the eaten multiplied in shadows hunchd in
audiences of shadows who still watch them 24/7 in
some empty skullTheater auras of stale nicotine
how we pass the time
                    if KnifeBoy sweats it tastes
like heroin,vinegar or wine &only a nightsweat in
our dreamtheater   otherwiseKnifeBoy is indifferent
here we are preNoon the performance thickens the
noise& afterburn we are not so beautiful in daylight
        /a city imagined a postDeath still functioning still a
crowd of apparences as if alive pragmatic things who
eat sense light erosion of bldgs as some script or gears
turn in them they do not recallBeing but a repetition

enactd among its ruins absently as you do not exit
night w/out paying the bill as the next day is the
preceding nights refill
                      time to go he sez
                      take it w/us

            * * * * ** * * *

they walkd north into IceCity *who are we when* back
and forth in my dreams the chronic sidewalks 800,000
bce *what time where* as shaggy dreamers Africa to Euro
all a trancd turf and then something is cold the ice walls
tall and silent bldgs adjust to time as chthonic wheels
as some gray overpass of sky over us *become an other
imagind thing* whatever works the earth happens
                      KnifeBoy goes east some
upscale woman w/a car he drives and too fast topdown
pretends to be in time w/a watch she gave him tictoc
on his opiate wrist & the sun is relentless drags its
heatlight over him he is always cool at yr peril
                      i walk around original barrios
brokenglass mercado a library one street w/shade from
whats left of once architectd life or an old house a tree
Chinese elm 2 women livd there thru window blinds
could see 1 everyday some gringa writer typing in her
middleagd underwear on that street kidnoise muted or
nowhere what did she ever record a museum life the
artefacts amusing think of their brownsexd gods he
laughd *oldcow* old typewriter dull underwear i walk
there to wonder if id ever been there or her
characteristically he will score return the car w/cunt
&or jism scent lingers a perfume she will kiss lick his
opium dick barechest the unslept eyelids avertd neck
indifference makes her come unlike a sun he rises
abruptly zips up whiteshirtblackshoes when will/*later*
wroughtirongate noon walled garden bushes grass
whats left dust a street east to west the suns hustle
                KnifeBoy does not like the cold he
is always cold some cow audumla scoopd us fromIce
like a kid lickd helados in the simple heat *who we are*
a restless boned people mythos of Fire&Ice conflictd
or salutrean Gravettian FrancoCantabrian i think we
were hunters & drew pictures a future walld by thick
ice as heroin,glass function to see more or less huge

emptied structures in my eyes that isTime he requires
heat mirage he shimmers it is all Illusion it sd watch
me magician walk asIf revelation is streetcon a gutter
bum a god whatever works as glacial crack boom
like a planet falls on a planet whatever changes
         i do not change but observe curious chemistry
of an eye watches history shedded from skin centuries
or eons altitudes temperatures geologic poems of all
regions my body passagd thru w/him he doesnt know
exceptNow he wants time fixt on his arm like a clock
blueink tattoo name naild to a sky oldstory old gods
move on he walks ½ drunk downtown winesweat cunt
or heroin eraser over sky of one more day i watch him
from a distance that never closes this isLove the lucent
glaze/gaze of knowledge over disaster what theEarth
knows no body wants to know a few bucks kills late
noon heat old rerun cinemas w/air conditiond by bad
actors b/w scripts our perfect scenarios dubbd in lost
tongues the balconies blow dreamsmoke over our
heads This is cool he sez im hungry there is always
desertd night returnd to maybe she gave/he stole cash
jewelry appetite for luxury sit outside cantina carne
seca beer coffee nobody else around old pleasures *what
comes next after this* i think 1000 years ago 2000 years
discourse panorama plague war famine etc Inquisition
theEnd again again   /*after this occurs after we are this*
nothing changes in fantasy (only)the machine advances
his metallic fix &sole need   hot cool
                           history exists as aJoke on us
continuous apart continuously a part partial of some 1st
equation i Inventd &then become *as we exist* lava,swamp
glacier shedded off to dust our present flesh ,hypnotic
bodies w/chilld eyes &humid genitals(ours)atmosphere
of earth as unavoidable   pulses &f(r)iction i cannot
enter fire or ice w/out him also it is/as in such veins
alchemically fixd

5
      the poet the whore the pimp have in common   a similar corner understood the Magician baggd w/desperate tricks out ofNothing i say snap! the city as ultimateVoyeur turns us out for entertainment you may watch too it is free   the imagination hustles things on the streets (there was)food drink styles of bodies noise everything pays its dues to something to belong also(it is not free)   i wear ripd jeans loose brown sweater no lipstick no femStink up my soild sleeve seduction it doesnt matter somedick always appears like weather whether or not yr trying or where you go next a bad dream

transactions   :over the night as animals (animals are gone the moon is gone)women hustle the hunters/hungers how many dirty fingers on their guns or shooting up yr cunt(Imagination is also real) so you move endangerd dangerous mysteried as last beast alive is wary of meatvalue   & *shines w/epiphany:* walk ahead of the guy slow down make him think some alley dumpster doorway ahead turn around in this hidden stare at him reach for fly already opend yr fist his bulgd flesh KB from behind coldcocks rip off watch wallet white dick stud or approx shoesize walk away not too fast his slurrd eyes attempting focus sees the ground w/puke close to his nose he will not follow we are night successful this opening act of darkness what next plunder blanks the eyes pimpboy needs a fix i cannotFix
                                      alone on the same street all time is fixed from moment to moment nobody knows if we are dead or not differences are material this is the same dream   i wanna fuck i wanna fuck guy maybe reincarnate or just redundant on the planet shovd up into my eyes eternal need pushd into me shiv of *do me do me* hes there im here as if owed what else is life good white guy maybe homeless hangs out hothours in the library or doesnt get clean in 24/7 laundromat or nothing cares not there allnite church cathedral govnt bldg parkinglots the civiccenter plaza fountain abandond of first waters the edible pigeons romantic at nite once after films concerts lectures date w/welldressd sex their moist parts bulges glamorously fixd/decoratd this guy comes at me w/ nothing what i owe him what guns are for slug w/mood bullets he slinks into the next cunt who doesnt exist for

him except xchange value he cant change it puts hmslf
to sleep somewhere jerksoff w/tears murderdreams the
nextdays dumpster(like a pillow it promises something)

the losers   :populate the planet women play their parts
sadistically bloodlips long starvd legs *razors cut their
thighs to be hurt fashionably* crashdEyes at intersections
remind them you are carnal when it explodes beasts
are gods as sacrificial food as daily fatal   /pieces all raw
invisible scenarios in yr skull   flashd glass reflections
for sale its yrs to kill
                           i watchd her(myself)as in dept
store window strippd sellingVibrator w/demonstrations
ofExstasy that is a real job on this hallucinatd corner the
trickhand is empty he sd *keep moving or stand there* &
all the animals come down to the waterhole to drink a
truce of thirst among beasts extinct here except women of
thin flesh prowld as *leopardskin tigervein snakecoil* ink
stain tattooed into them   by their own hand/for the thrill
          let me be yr wetdream shoot me up
i stand in a bare room woodfloor open window hot
dirtyard outside treeshade 112degrees some latenoon
breeze or someone breathing a pornfilm open garage
other side of alley men hangout there throw dice cards
beer smoke the air nicotine or honest sweat imagind
where i stand just heat beats down rises up breathes
in & out a slow trance rhythm im naked the garage
can see a ghostwhite body one hand twisting nipples
fingers into my cunt play w/the hairy folds the clit
arousd by them watching they know this anonymous
men i dont want to know them they will get hard as
they finger their cards roll zigzag the porno distance
in their dark eyes fantasize man stares into window
i splay my cuntlips push it toward him he can never
get in i can make him wish to enter his tongue he
pushes his tongue into it fingers the skin vulvafolds
around & around they watch in the garage hot w/
arousal but will never move beyond this distance i
will do it again each day the sexd heat cannot stop

we are inside glass,something glassy heroin airspace
surrounds yrbody finally naked not to touch except as
merchandise/illusion a mannequin of hard stares
pricetag dangld from her cunt   *once*

*softbodied women the cars inject them w/some blue
hype hypnotic liquid substance of somedream they
floatd in advertisements of themselves   i watch them
surrender veins opend to cynical rust a chemical flush
rush of past histories into this terminal skinflags flutter
in hallucinatd wind*
      women with tattooed skin& painted teeth   Baudelaire, the Voyage
magicians who could make great snakes appear
i can decorate night w/them obviously (animals are
gone the moon is gone)
      we cant help it we just are
there is a doorway middleagd woman who writes w/
a knife &a blackpen in her pocket her name is Eva
of Germanic origin as her eyes fixd on the words as
words leave her brain into her stiff arm the compelld
pen dimlit flattend notebook pages rarely crossd out
correctd discourse (the)saga(cious) or not(noone
reads it)theme via her long isolation/to(isolate)enter
an eventual sewer she knows this as teutonic history
often dwells on such accurate memoir asScience or
doomd she observes this homelessness in a world
toilet her privacy where a mind runs out (one day)
one word at a time or black rune mapping a paper
of her experience doomd but literate it is not new
here as in other ancient vigils there is no last line she
writes there is no perfect end she keeps the knife
sharp or legendary no body comes close or ever wd
want altho i wonder if its a poem
               /*or once were as strange moths
fleshmoths huntd nightlong for yr colors strategies of
staind alleys explode the delicate powders each
attemptd wing of eons as fragile inevitable as you
are*   words do not believe themselves here
Eva not a lover we are voluspa stared thru fatal air
womanly we see before &After orgasms apocalyptic
original gardens are of War,grenades of stars lurid
flowers spectacular extinctions go off random as gods
play their game no rules,unruld immortalPrecision or
men or boys fire spermshot exotic ordinance orderd
ordinary orders this is the warrior beyond words we
see sereTime *the nude petals,bodies tropic to poetry
twistd undone* how Machines play you will escape
permittd only by mechanicalEye,a rapturd gun
          willingly to be beautiful as to surrender

what never was but pushd into them images ofDesign
neon pulse of vulvas irreducible off/on a sad song sd
iridescent in oild gutters as a lip torn glossy w/blood&
lost language women are old news timeblown against
obedient sewers   what she writes down is known   *i
was once young distributed in pieces windowslash of a
face as not sweet enough or alone or circumstance or
last chance deploy what i become this is the trash of
pain* /fragmentd islands in a terrible river menstruald
from earthend center soppd up in her bad poems (she
writes crouchd in a doorway *deepwords* Insane)as
subcutaneously flowBiohologivrams of worldly cunt he
drills in his sleep her iron(y)as *otherwordly poems*
& here a parade going by of killers&sleek tanks gods
engines returnd from worldsend w/manufacturdSirens
omniscient debris of brokeGutterals *what Eva records*
as slow procession of steel across a throats roar(her
singingknife)chrome rampd polishd skratch of fingerd
nails *my wheels enter avenues of female skulls* armor
bearing names of all the wild dead animals

she is tall chubby her brains fuckd at birth 17yrs old
now 65IQ adolescence spent riding citybus sideseats
for disabld/elderly people all day like watching tv the
people get on the bus pass by her gaze once followd a
curiosity now gazes into some space before her eyes
or a cattlegaze looking for some other thing beyond
feedlot stall slaughterramp i project this some torment
in her eye vacancy other years sat in cutoff jeans legs
open unaware did not care nobody thought intentiond
sometimes pubichairs showd desire to be a teenager
w/healthy legs a happiness of animals downtown in
homeless camps tribes of adolescents she let them
play w/her pussy in rumors night down by the dry
river she feels shes beautiful she thinks they love her
ie she belongs is happy let it be 3 years later on a bus
same sideseats longpants down to fat ankles thongs
filthy feet not dirt but the blackdust of streets tires oil
her jersey shirt green bluish yellow color of nausea
vaguely watches bodies movements episodes around
her alone sunk in used flesh(i project this)a few blocks
she gets off lumbers lost into some downtown room
or streethustle or little storefront of soul salvation
they might feed her or know her name

(as if)
    naked in my circumstance the scent of no money
charity in the crotch &earthbrains heatd on a trigger
like kill is love behind you the corner at busstops a
terminal doorway i wanna fuck you ill fuck u   i am
a poet in my skin therefore i belong poets are born
in the flesh we write of
                everything you see determind by money
everythingplacedaynight theres a #number# on yr
forehead not of a beast not 666 animals dont do money
the human beast is money the human beast apotheosis
is money it evaluates yr soul it finds you wanting it
finds you now wanting everything it will no longer
allow you to have let u have
      =you dont count =deal w/it =shut up
shovd in yr mouth like a dick   *shut up*
killers are born in the flesh written off

we are comfortable here at home the impervious ice
remembers us :return to glass it says (remote as the
invention of runes)
who is Eva EvaVoluspaVolva amnesiad battles in a
warrior brain *writing it down* or mss in a desert well
preservd   we flamed in our own books(or myths of)
gringo writer in her sane underwear risible thru gaped
window Eva in a doorway writes archival things she
may or may not remember in this afterburn the little
altars of VirginMotherWhore framd their pale bodies
vacatd of everything but ritual desire the air is thick
w/it no wonder they worship a cathedral vulva born
from returnd to never leave it dip fingers in the holy
smeard juice on the tongue around mouth yr torso liftd
swelld convulsd the swoon of godlust everyone knows
is sexd the metaphorical is one *Urth is Wurd is Wyrd*
we flamed in our own books (or myths of) :there was
a poem illusiond a godtrick crazy women burnd in our
alembic metaphors
those of us who come hard are doomd to be romantic
i think Eva is writing the history ofTime the Western
worlds invention of clocks Doomsday god as deadline
guillotine punishment for a lifespan begins & ends in
some crime Ragnarok ends then begins again this
guillotine never ends its sudden fall /eclipse *again*
      its supposd to hurt thats how you know its real

it is a dark urinatd stairwell in a building abandond
by time it is a wall of piss and shadows he sits on the
bottom stair w/his fly open his penis is a dead animal
in this building i stand above him he wants it i stand
on the 6th stair above him he wants to tell me what to
do i wear tight pants then a skirt then pantyhose then i
am nude below wearing a tshirt i concentrate my clit
pulsd in his thought his fuckfinger raisd up over his
right shoulder
now do it w/this finger he said i likd to see that he was
shaking as he watchd me rub myself according to his
direction he had no control but illusion dont come he
said but i did then he had to wait all in imagination
he stares at the wall pissd bottom of a stairwell hes
never turnd to watch my finger in my pussy as he
wants commands thus we prolong eternity pass the
smoke pass the time   beyond glass:
it is a dark urinatd stairwell try to sit smoke or nod
off heat blast beyond is painful the stink as perfume
aura of this time radiant from 5dimensions up/down
sideways in/out survival consciousness delirium now
the greatDoors open executioner enters,robot camera
            im going crazy here
   alone w/in elevator suit briefcase never glances looks
upward at ceiling at his watch at his futureSuccess in biz
always behind me always machinery of flesh& progress
his brain the same wanna fuck wanna fuck u as the street
man the alleyman the habitue of our gutter but its less
immediate violation of pub(l)icspace of my body his
interior fantasy more american psycho his wetcream if
nobodys around and he can beat you to death after 4am
yr soild underwear or hiz(s)mother or yr attitude leaks
out contempt a political act he hordes himself only it
doesnt belong to U nothing digs condom out of yr
dying cunt leaves the elevator   right on Time cueExit
removing his gloves i watch this movie in his suave
skull going down to the ground floor descending to
the morning where we both get out greet the day

it is a dark urinatd stairwell try to sit smoke or nod
off heat blast beyond is painful the stench as perfume
aura of this time radiant from 5dimensions up/down
sideways in/out survival consciousness hot delirium
            recurrent this scene repeats repeats you

repeat   the redundance separates me out
>   im going crazy here
>   i dont know how to breathe w/out
you (moron) more on this later as the nite closures
in close suffocatd spasm of all yr versions reductio ad
absurdum or who invented language mustve known
>   how to breathe here   how to breathe
its supposd to be alive thats how you know its Life
>   those of us dontCumEazy doomd to beRomantick
:the classic elevator
i can go all the way to the top & go down in the same
breath

* * * * * * * *

introduce me to yr Sex knifeBoy how it has become
masterFull
   a weapon condensd from night explodes the night

daily businessman enters rooms w/alien shades drawn
to visit w/the dark something enters retro night to fuck
w/its stars   what is the soul of systems machines that
glow like flesh and nude bodies pawnd like typewriters
in broken shops w/stopt clocks and their proprietors
cannot fix all the junk you bring in
> *whoever built a system*
to visit w/the darkest rooms a gun holster lies on the
bed like a child or rooms reservd for solitude he cold
fucks to populate w/another body or rooms he sez are
not his business only dreams   rooms she enters on
a tray &they lick small bones clean shuffle her like a
pack of cards in staind fingers mean rooms where sex is
rushd thru gangveins thru genital mobs that rule night
bored w/all this   bodies are spread magazines
that sweat like coins or hours where women voyage
on the tongue to paradise braincells where nerves are
whips and bootheels fellatios of beggars cells where
the gray moon scratches her name and number on a
cold wall everything is empty in this place imprisond
w/our bodies   dawn a pile of bones mountd
on a skyline assemblages of lips &hair smeard over
leadsolderd sun from obscene high windows reptilic
voyeurs look down at porno lines of workers acts of
sadoservice uniforms w/breasts arrest strippd women

*they are searchd for razors bread brains poems fear
bodies fuck &grind each other in daylight like rentd
gears &the point is these are jobs payment to live on
a planet   yr neat face fastend in white stacks at the
office this is a good job yr labia spreadsheetd graphd
stockd inventoryd businessmen are eunuchs feral
moans in the musak pheromones sprayd in scrotal
cubicles whatever sells this dickshit
 it is from Time inheritd from crotches of ratalleys it
starts out w/mercy ends up wanting yr face dead no
mercy in the bankvaults where it is lockd up no nice
thing in salttears piled up on cargodocks flavord w/
prettycolors boxes of artificial tits tight slimed holes
stackd shippd highjackd on the high pornographic
sea rotten w/spoild food bloatd fish   zones of it
beyond nations beyond worlds where factories make
perfect flesh and the air is hot pink w/its redundant
ecstasy yr torso tattood w/fuckads location of yr bare
room famineextinctionplans killstrategies unfoiling
from international crushd and plush cunts i cd go
on   what is the soul of systems the need of
lost girls the vanity of poor bitches the elegance and
truth of whores who open to jisms of engines and the
real dollar   what is the
soul of systems blood flows coldly like a fishtide
corpses of men that leak oil take a thousand years
to die*

a stray gray kitten they find in a barn bring it home the
small female dog takes it in nuzzles it in 3 days begins
to make milk lactates &almost purrs w/it tell me what
kind of earth this is the original creator of yrBrain

lets say U forgot entirely who are where from reason
4being (none) you say Nothing became you & now
regrets the trip

KnifeBoy taps his blade on the glass or its the light
cutting yr eyes sometimes dawn sometimes not the
variant thought of this place confusd in its dreams
     i think its him on the other side wanting in hes
dead he always wants in a knife can do it it writes
on yr skin *or else*

knifeBoy was a poet once on proprioceptive earth
        who wuznt he sez times are tough get yr
ass ready im a businessman   [he sez]

    a downtown motel we are meant to go there,beige
walls dirty carpet beige brownyellow papery drapes
the blinds never see the drapes never open something
on a bed never washd enough to not remember the
showerstall toilet sink chippd medicinecabinet empty
mirror empty lucky toiletpaper a few towels one glass
if not enough one thirst if not enough tv w/all the bad
shows you want to stare at &never think .about it all
the stink of cunt it must be me   20bucks for a nights
sleep it is so easy to earn   Eva should come
to watch 3rdEye of the magician in the forehead of a
timeclock on a nighttable beside the theatrical bed if
you were spread wider,Night cd dreams become real
how does it feel sdNight   nothing to it
    *sirensnarld w/silence yr electric eyes are
druggd like every animal dilate or shrunk to the fix as
leanbellied cars cruise veins of boulevards who rides
in their uterine vacancy of us*   10men for a 24hr fix
it is easy to burn or stonecold fall from a void w/out
celebration act like you love it like you love me sez
KnifeBoy beer pizza tv its just a business no wonder
they grow tired of flesh as flesh as if anAlchemy had
faild i am a fixture a juicy furniture or simulate some
burststar in dim memory of a world love it if you love
me sezKnifeboy nobody gets killd   &then it
works because it works,kicks in scratch cocaine on a
cervix like writingFire on ice explode her into aCosmos
where she is at least at home   *knifeboy knows this*
        a cloud of origins becomes me
before it matters before its lost andEva comes to watch
  andEva comes to watch
    Eva comes into the world to watch motelroom or
church or wherever mortals sink to their knees to give
head or money or submit Fear to god dont hurt us dont
hurt us nothing id want to be here iven if it cd sdEva
writing down into the worlds dark thought
     Eva theButch squat not sexd every season of the
same suitjacket trousers black navy heavy&dull in the
groin of heat croppd brownish dull hair man eyes who
wants to think her cunt nothing to explore except her

face always looks down concentratd on paper where
words appear like she follows them w/her ballpoint like
a secretaryDictation who wd go there want to be that
she never seems to sweat
Eva theButch nonbeautiful her own wetdream motel of
girls(killers)in her mind negotiates w/pimps,junk she
wants things too Tall thin indifferent ones (who)cant
care fuck yr feel/cd care less what fingers dicks pubic
tongues romantikGermantik bitchbrain/Valkyrie gang
crotchd on their deathhorses in her head in yr bed in
my deadend arm   torture me i will come

                      what is this for   only
aMagician attends a performance ofTrueRomance an
illusional presence mirage of essence that it is merciful
(always) no (but yet) capable of magic tricks asEarth
is for as anonymous fucks alive rancid in the skin of
my bed   (i live) we are alone KnifeBoy &me curld
up w/(in)/Mother the original whore
                           what this is for

    a body fixd w/faint contusions of stars or appears
    like illumination in bleak windows
    was it deals of muscle tossd eyes nipples menstrual
    history thru the hard beds spots of oil on the
    fleshsheets that wont wash out
    body fixd w/anemones and velvet bruises female
    body who slides like ice along the tides tangled groin
    maps of murder on violet fingernails that cut and
    lose you leaving no crime
    but moon like blurry foam on a blue-inked mouth
    voyeurs everywhere one profession of aHomeless planet
    satellite voyeur my pimp mon frere stares of enucleatd
    windows videos of shadowy rigs perform lewd &weird
    movements&contracts unobserved retinal deals who
    want to see thru flesh into the agony absolute stare
    who watches us seek who is watching us grope the
    dark
        what is the soul of systems in a luminescent ocean
    where eels and sharks entangle to digest the dark

    this is hizPoem knifeBoy delicate in his cold heart
    fixd w/needles he likes needles he needs to be a girl
    sometimes he fucks himself this is the history of the

world nobody does it better than a boy in such deep
selflove
god he is cruel
everything not me everything in the world is not me
curld up in his sea knifeclutchd indifferent for the kill
thePimp is always a girl foetal in his sex he knows how
it feels & heatseeks revenge (profit,prophet of what
is to cum   ) what is Sukcess he asks exactly
    bombs of hard orgasms this is a real war now
'La lutte des sexes est le moteur de l'histoire.' /Robbe-Grillet, Djinn, pg 19/
corporate night[he sez]embodied night as the original
like my mother fuck her games rank w/her aloneness
    you sez those fishy parts we hook men like jeezus
not amusement solace justice just pain is bizness this
is a lovestory she sez trueromance of it ofUs *endless*
curld up in foetal blackness history i am business

      * * * * * * * * *

thePoet the pimp my cunt   impatient for action here
. knife boy   -out of her dreams a necessity someone
to discourse w/between suicides
metaphysical*Urth*One   is it All one   wonderfull who
won   molten &rare acidic our membranes burn/pay
xtra i will bite what tender night   what plague what
entertainment who knows   a thought extrapolatd
from night occupies the night   like we occupy a room
.Time is anonymous   so is the room   so is yr name
asEva writes it down   :extract the *need* once
open real   animal bone massive &serious in itsEpic
prowl female& male in naked hunger did it make this
game(in the end)whoever plays   *whatKnifeboy says*
.no mates but habits no Universe but machine no
    original planet noBody belongs to .*as if* a home
no lovers but assassins mercenaries of a mind feverd
to destroy its kind o exotic(juice)ofMind   *you bitch*
unkind *yr kind*   .i see us costumd as sex(uncookd)
meat inExchange weXchange for the beasts all gone
*we are not gone we are beastly machines now you
made us asGods*   .you may stalk ourExistence its
just bizness   *ok ok let us repeat this*   in
trancd busyness of flesh   *not again o fuck* the*fuck*
misery of time displacd by rapture *fuckin lightchangd*
that is precisely the point of discourse

*/ out of her dreams a necessity someone to imagine
w/between suicides /*
yr emptied eyesBlink
closed opend   ask me if i comprehend the Irony
   a *mystery* (quantum performance daily)something
about theUniverse just stringing us along   he sez   (not
really)the show continuums
   an animal expanded from night implodes the night

get yr ass ready

theVulva speaks

    :is a different earth   as describd   in a mirror i am
corpseblue & hellish pink,that neon glow of fluorescing
worms as described   document of alleys as they
pulsate ,stink of useful   eating & mantic morphism   calld
decay   still i work here   teeth,bones rust or also
a blue radiation   she comes to repeat autopsy labs& motel
rooms of their   processes
       a strange planet estrangd planet   in a mirror i am
silent as
usual observe them as wormborn   crawld of corpse eyes
or a brain of raw inside that juicd off,manganese feral
oxides poem effusions   clay fungusd as flesh sideways
then eruptd   my thoughts   is the smell   as long thighs
into a cunt,mushroomd   uterus of root brain as fungus of
bodies
is   built inside,out   exponential deathtaught lifetaut this
agaric/homokaryotic   tongue   it means to breathe,gilld
&of one origin   some thick
smell of earth was   always   it means we live a tongue
thick w/it of fluorescing words
         we livd or went mad,berserkers inside
the huge sex organs of all horizons
                        delirium ,of
flies inside my head   the shamanic transport a form of
mosquitoes attacking,rodents bugs scatterd   visions
in the alleys of   decay,maggot messages of   yr flesh as
experimental   residues   as poetry   is from

:as describd   descried in a mirror   she utterd   once
planet utterance,   heard tongue
                        i forget

      _____   *the nigredo* _____

they wanted me on motel bed,arms strapped down legs
spread opend cunt so id get hot they hung out,beer pot
tvporn background   fucktalk   sound   punches of laughter
heard into all surrounding night the dark is alive here w/
shittalk among brotherhoods   i am extension of the
scene or cheap furniture,wellused   i stare at ceilings &
hear the ambience of hemispheres   similarly employd
this is a world   KnifeBoy   grows old   will become

old,subject of dying   the lovedeath of my kind he
hasnt read the   books, i dont think

---

it doesnt hurt

---

                        as in a cave human,animal
hunger   *a gangrene luminesce of the brain* any animal
becomes human   and we became   human,any
animal becomes its food in the imagination of a hunger
evolve   electric eyes rapacious lights sexy &void in a
primevil city a million years a hairy body is gives birth in
a cave a basement of bloodrags &human bones gnawd of
animal bones animal bones chewd of human bones it is
cold &the traffic goes thru yr veins like ecstasy for the
last nite hungrily a million years the brain grows
                the hunger inside *ravenous of thought
of memory these 2 leave worldsedge on my black wings*

            in my skull this occurs *nox profunda* deliberate
the toxicMagician,his fleshy drums bone rattles obscene
in body cavity It dances hunger as dream,stenchd alembic
potions the naked couple who will be torn apart & melted
down for body parts who will be joind then dissolvd &
solved again or do they ever say No refuse to *remember*
this every piston ramrod ironbar into yr flesh forging
the illusion this is Love,he sez the mysterium of erotic
hunger the noise is going by outside like war,celebration
far away faroff their hologram ofWorld   happens
                                    / the corpse
who knows it dies but will not relinquish,hunger a motel
room a cave yr holy brain the decoration of visible space
w/us as same space of a cauldron pubicmoss floats oil
in stonedish yr eyesockets flckerd walls of dark/light as
in a church w/hypnotic bodies the devotional aspect of
animals(bison stag ox horses grotesque women)ritualizd
caverns as we never changd from this yr god yr art yr
hammerd machinery of thought what does he need this
magnetic hunger for what to return to what my body of
the solitary beginning   *let them in let them in*
      inaccessible in clefts deep colorous galleries innard
earth all the paints running down my nerves as visions of,
i see you on the street as cannibals hunt raw merchandise

i inventd this all my lavish illustrations &mythic acts
black echoes of a skull enlargd by meat piercd of delicate
chippd point by blood streakd across the eyes and brains
suckd out thru a small precise hole *it doesnt hurt* i
have inventd this ecstatic pain all these curld up in the
belly the stink of bowels as blackearth stinks in the
alchemical theater   here we are
                    yr fingers enter me as a voyage thru
the dark i know it ends here
                              (she watches,Eva watches us
the necessary spectator Inquisitor of histories)my body
floats interior seas i am the sea   shapes of her fingers
inkd &silent *she writes* horn,bone lunar hooks the moon
glows of large hollow eyes as *requird observer* slowly
herds move in limestone walls over mountain passes&
grass plains their eternal flesh shines like thought on the
hunters retinas,i in the largest cave turn haunches of blue
scars thru nites of long spears teeth chewing etchd tattoos
as maps of great passage over dreamd territory   over
& over we saw this in a movie time passd for us
       shaman in a hungertrance that feeds on all this
can you remember before it was war it never was

/all my colors melting down back to earth the maggot
mouths open for us cut yr tongues& wrists my red white
yellow black absolute paints dissolvd down surfaces as
faces sprayd utterances spells against the hallucinatd
wall melt run down some whores mascaraed skin the
creases gutters in her biography she knows well /
/eva feeds on all this   *eva is a bottomless well*

---

subterranean hair mattd clots beastskulls slept in funk
basement staind rise/fall of stairways w/animal noises
bodies herds of bodies thru shiftd walls move flowerd
dresses thru forests glassd paintd eyes bare arms mouths
wipd of red hands the dogs the horses the sorcerer the
naked women gesture on a small screen on acrid mind
stared into other lives vicarious scripts of optd being
shapes of knives cuts of lean meat dimensiond on white
plates moon opaqued the hungers of napkins of revvd
motors of lipstick of starving chairs hungers of ancient
drivers of thin herds thin bodies risen climbd to static

*rooms where dim lamps echoic skulls perform primal
rites flesheaters draw opiate fingers along yr soft throat
bone split w/siren cries the bending saxophone jazzd
&fuckd by every century in yr veins dissolvd orgasm
of a brain evolvd by tongues evolvd by blood &erotic
terror music&beauty suckd in and out anonymous holes
eternal darkness strewn w/picked bones on the thick
carpet where footprints still mark slowdances dream
moving thru corridors thru huge windows into night on
tides of a great sea the cockroach the rat the shivery
whore as pimps w/spears smeard in spine marrow as
hidden sleeping in roots of eyelashes blurrd w/tears of
magenta &oil nude earth in a large swoon exposes its
belly to mouths of starvd stars magis drunk on famine
shadows pass in and out doors a trance of endlessness
fall on us w/mouths of no edges swallow all this*

---

      watch us Eva,voyeur watching as eating brains
raw,other brains rich in nutrients of terrestrial knowledge
such sustains the cruelIce marks the body staind,tattoos
of virtual bodies stains us w/insane skill genius of the
kill,our Art (she watches)
      the eyes are immense in the skull reverently crossd
2femurs inside a bearskull as a power to be a god who
is real who awes w/presence real asHunger from raw
fingers as fire becomes illuminate of this darkly bottomd
cavern we see inside our futures powers of beasts upon
walls   the needle on the blanket is ancient the stitch the
fix warm rush to the brain of this gnawd chewd animal
who eats the world as if born ravenous inside it still
bloodfed by a long loopd cord   the lariat noose ring of
coniunctio alchemica
                   eating brains that dream evolves
the dream   Exponentially

---

this is what we made KnifeBoy the *ecstatic union* like
knife into flesh loud crash of planets at intersections so
predictable disillusion of,illusion of
& every ramrod piston rebar into the cunt a world can
imagine cauldron of spectacular agon/pain *theatrum
chemicum* all transformation an end of boredom or what
cannot be born or the unbearable my pelvis as a bear

skull staring of the black earth,night

it doesnt hurt   because i submit to this   necessary
solve et coagula
    Eva for the 1st time wears a dress,long black priestly
robes torturous rapes are in her dungeons the schoolgirl
notebooks   prisoner notes   this is the
religion of her dreams

it doesnt hurt   or it is epic pain the same thing

---

thru some window beyond   gray sky   yr
                                          emptied eyes

there is gray sky as if nite ends   night does not end i
inhabit a crevice in rock magic& alone florescent(as)
grafitti in some alley Eva writes this poem a grave is
eyelevel w/passing hooves or sleepwalkers ghosts thru
my anthropomorphoid   dream
    /oil dropt on original waters   how we are colors   the
        amazing colors were of our   eyes/
who were you now you have returnd   . darkness

          i have dreamd it out of this body thru its
glassy windows the dark real of night the wheels rolling
inside me metallic&dissolving of any face ofTime i wd
know it by   you float out the window if there are eyes
or windows apertures the room is a camera the aperture
a gods cunt   you are born
        what is a body   a structure,a place to live,
building in time   a void w/doors or elevators in&out
of flesh portals if it cd be it cd not be or tunnel or sewer
between the worlds(the)funnel of stars of terminal escape
explosions out of this *what is it for*   solve et coagula i
inventd this   sulfurous orgasm   suicide to be real
          corpsd there on smell of black earth the
keme chyma sheets of layers of pits of chasms of   need
it doesnt hurt or is numb cold frigid not there inside the
fire that does not burn   *menstruum*   its mothers dark
blood or oceanic flux of *she needs   to pass time*

    what is a body it is what we us(e) to become this
monstrous of metal,visionary glass cold ash arisen foam,

mysteries fluidfire stablewater elixir of desire jismd &
cunt sludge eat shit drink piss tears sweat &the fingers
in my cunt my anus & they are the priests fingers the
interrogative fires of godslust i excite as if another
        what it was to be   of a beginning
    (in yr cloudy placenta built of all of this)
the ashtree Yggdrasil worldtree of a nervous system,it
grew upward thru coils into my black ravenous hair &
absolute stare ofEyes into terms of being *rapturous*
all i wantd the beautiful Other variants of a cruelty
was i a girl ever who didnt know thisChemistry as it
makes us up&down the spine of,scaffolding urges of
welding,hammers *what are you making* it is Love he
sd iron rod piston rebar into yr orifaces   consider
our mutual agonies,splicd & forever   *a history*
he is pushing some juice of earth into his arm,fucking
his vein for warm,flowering reasons not to see them
ugly   they are banging to enter their tomb or some
cloudy penthouse in the tower of herMind what does
he need this hunger for what raptorous(black shining
night)architecture,room of fuck   we live in

---

                    he is gone

---

as edges of mossy rocks a wet green sheen *imagination
exudes from it black earth* a body exuding thoughts thick
exudation sweat of all this plenitude
               this is a love experience our chemic
effusion shoot me w/coherent light i will do it all again

             my sensations,Eva writes her fingers in
my cunt,anus mouth &they are the poetic fingers the
interrogative flare of godlust i exhibit calld Love,&great
arts inquiringBeauty &the great Body of some thing that
is beautiful   as Her fingers enter it
                    and they are all numb
how did i kill you over&over it is appearance until it
grows redundant   ,numb

how do i kill him   cease to imagine   him

abominations they sd or greatWealth orHel ,industrial

erotic forgeries of design& destiny *saltfleshd & he
sweatd wine* consider this,deliberate the usages of him
congeald light earthy sun gold metals colors &glass of,
*misogynd boy who is halfgirl girlselffuckd a godpimp
metalnaked poet all his alchemical glory of my dark
bed* the oxymorons all exhibitd among them you are
crouchd hunchd ,fetally curld enjoying bliss yr open
mouth drooling as a cavernous spring,infant water

      Magician,as he sleeps

Eva meanwhile,some motelmaid at the door we cleanup
(human)laboratories every bed the magnificent fuck of
nights volcanic factories,igneous ooze & most of all an
Ecstasy paid for ,recognition of,original sensate primal
pulse suck sex feces piss menstrual birthblood heat fear
fist gun smashd bottle knifefuck into yr   reality
  breathing   must be repeatd
          must be repeatd
how do i kill him   cease to imagine this

       this is a love experience Being
pimpd out by its own Creation   /subordinant properties
(male)(time)(restlessness)(consequence)(desiredesire my
need)(lostness)or as you want the sea,or a desert or iceSex
do you want the sea or spectacular __ Sex do what fix in
yr brain explode universe in the next one better than this
do you see a ship shivvd into sand this desert drives the
nothing flesh deep bottom of yr throat where jism is whats
left of ocean is there any consequence to this a thin pale
diminishing sidewalk like water running out ghostheroes
leap from the stuck hull in the shape of legendary rats do
you want a urinal a cathedral do you want
              a home/
   your nose looks frozen and your eyes are dead
many colors just before we die   i burst as yr eyes   ice
over or become fire   there is saltsweat,& water you do
not cry like a human but like a   terminal rat
          as i lovd you

---

     the bitch is rolling all over the floor the
stupid evidence of Aloneness this is a Universe
  what is it for there was a desert there was ice a
sea covered the primal street once in fathoms of silent
& omnivorous commerce among the fish the sharks the
technicolor whores always flashy in the inkd depths
  always the skirt lifts the legs part the mouth swallows
  you whole the hole is aMouth disappears ocean &
Universe in one big *suck*   Replay this
now the bitch is rolling all over the floor of the galaxy
  3 times i have burnd thru windows of ice in
bondage to bad movies on the screen of yr fixd eyes &
as he burnd me in brotherhoods ofInquisition orgies of
alchemical fixes experiments ofChange i do not die

   what is original on a tvscreen in a funkd motel room
after midnite   i do not die except boredom
     evidence of a universe bored
on a bed of fire she transmogrified many bizarre &
te*rrible things issued from her serpent cavern spidery
slimey hissing &then hawks& howling animals &then
     women,& the possibilities of men*
— how did you end up this way KnifeBoy
— whatever works he sd
  in a bed of fire she (be)comes Gold came out of us &
strange creatures,KB crushd coal as thick black blood
gushd from wells &pores of transmorphd earth pain lust
came out of us &supernal creatures transfixd &metals
wept w/glorysheen more beautiful than you
     he can only be what i need
     he can only be what i am ritual of rushd
adrenaline, absolute imagination fractalling into all my
phantoms,surrenderd powers to their wild device all
aroundEarths sleep this bed of flames &repeatd ice &his
metallic indifference achievd he cd care less
  as prophesied   repeat,repeat replay this
— how did you become this way KnifeBoy
between cannibals &machines,the pimp &godgangs as
all these stories of cosmetic& realEvolution between
what is a choice betweenUs i am tired
      as prophesied
— you askd for it   the
drunk poets(as)if earth laughs gets drunk isYou you
asIf the mythology cartoon boobs&legs&Quest you

are representational or a symbolic act   Earth theShe
on stage strips down to nothing but the final question
who cares you think   its an old joke after all
           mechanical things impact yr uterus,ores or
other babies extractd from words accumulatd bruises
levels exspelld of ancient runes you know recall from
bottoms of a glass or streets of fathoms of remorseless
garbage   /mumbld sexsweat as a sad&sweet thing/

'...the universe,...is a machine for making gods...'   —Henri Bergson

it is dark.one body lies on another.clouds of blackish
grayish muscle surrounds them and yellowish light.
one body lies on another prevarication of a night i
cannot believe he was my fix aCosmic need orSpirit
wrestling deadweight lifting he does something
w/yr night
— how did you do it KnifeBoy
— reiteration   Time   drugs
the uterus is a machine for making gods   the brain is
a machine for making gods *godz R us* god isLust god
is yr Ice descending on my hotflesh we do not know
the labor involvd in this deliberate spectacle it evolves
us   we do not know the desire evolvd in this sadistic
spectacle it involves us
                          it multiplied
— repeat,Time   yr imagination
a pure description of night who has a body but it is
everywhere ultimate black spill from bones marrow
of stars into streets theyre made of the flesh of stars
&

———————————

how did you get to be you KnifeBoy
— its a cruel world
how did you get to be MechanicalGirl
— it was alone

———————————

he cd only be as i need some answer beyond
this stupid evidence aloneness is aUniverse garbage
eating bitch spikeheels dancd on glassyEmptiness :
broken in search of her inner whore   *what it is for*
        / focussed attention of mantic energies /
retinal burn i stard at fire you cut yr tongue for words

they used to do it on altars for gods   now in crackd
lots between void bldgs   his hallucinatory grandeur as
ador(n)d in   mescal powers
        i am naked(myself)(here)
mothers milk is a gateway drug galactic milk sprayd
sprays out of it into yr mouth you are a star or space
inside cannot forget   feeling   it seemd important
                       & visions
consumd in humanflesh or cookd women a holy feast
of consciousness an agony the priest devours&blesses
w/greasy fingers   cannibals,machines thePimp &god
gangs what choice he gives me what i want apparently
a drama ofTime   *to feel,in time*

drug by slow truck over the desert tied to trailer hitch
naked scarrd face breasts back thighs w/rocks cactus
spikes,shards of glass stuffd in her mouth,cunt shreded
ass for a freakfuck   leave her sprawld on park grass
dislocatd legs both shoulders twistd neck as a dry sun
of commerce comes up men gather to appr(a)ise the
displayd holes   is she viable   as a joke *what is it for*
              there are Valkyries they were furies i rode
as aBeast on aBeast valorous asHel to her lovers bed
Metis, pregnant inside Zeus' head, bangd metalwork
to build armor for Athena her incubating daughter,so
the clamor gave Zeus a headache so Hephaestos the
oreforger split open the god's head w/an ax & lo!
Athena wuz born, sprung forth fully grown & battle
armd the metal toughening her placental skin too bad
she was a fink for the boys,the gangs of Law&Order
they tie you down in some ratty motelbed & read u
theHolyLaw & whores of Babylon rode dragons if
horses not around,asBeasts we became religion or not
at all,you do not eXist except   cautionary moral,&
yr armpits ofHel,asBeasts hairy we mountd &rode out
warriors berserkers as any man when requisite,flaunt
of blood no problem when did that become
                              mythology
this slippage ofTime on the screen   ,exemplary &
technoColored atmosphere of my surrender i give it
upLove to yr huge& glamorous cameras,walls&every
eye the ceilings,mirrors that dont look back   &
others populate yr fantasy   randomly   it is
all a BigAct for the camera in the brain   he sd *such*

is the cosmology of the Void
    i followd him around as ifTrance as we
multiplied the desertd world voided its realness &our
vague eyes like gods abstractd time from its suffering
otherwise of course i feel every thing that is the point
ofBeing until redundant i am spread thin a film over
everything exhaled/exhalation as final comment or im
another woman just one more cagd here w/monsters
i imagind/creatd in original powers   *4 we luv the
drama*   sd the lipstick spit on theWall

they used to do it in dungeons for God,hiz porno lots
between void bldgs all the dead animals strewn around
carcasses randomly offering fastfood freelunch for
humans,maggots strange animals back beforeTime
came to tarpits,quicksand zoologic consciousness of
their planets appetite for them (how we did innocent
supermarkets you stroll out w/stashd meat in yr pants i
get searchd in the checkout candybars gumpacks in
my hands w/cash,nothing to hide
                      but i act tricky,mysterious)
                                      i dont
get it sez Nellie she is a ghost all this for what a *triste*
aspect of you or animal extinctions,w/my eyes gougd
out or visit me in a zoo,&my kid wanders into empty
museums crying mommy   you bitch.tell me what its
for   scatterd cinderblocks w/human shit depositd in
them they are toilets in the rubble everything stinks
of piss& vomit,puke &creosote saturates the air &
there is Nellie ghostbody splayd out in the vacantd
dustyard an old fastfood container the stain of grease
&blood salsa quickFix remains   salivant,alive
    Nellie,26-7, tall 1/2Mex w/blue eyes hung silent
w/them,shy her pimp her 2yearold brown boy they sd
she burnt them on a drugdeal ,draggd her into a dusty
backyard beat her unconscious one eye shovelld from
its pale socket,mouth clownderangd she didnt die but
some vegetable brain left, she movd hunchd up w/an
emptied face skullrings &burnt craters pockd,like the
fists that beat on her face made theMoon,it watchd &
stard a new face into her scard her kid when he saw
it,removd screaming Nellies gone eye forgot mirrors
so she had now no looks,no pimp no gang no home
no means of taking care,or brains to speak of as a

human should speak recall me,it sd(theMoon)we are
now one as aspects of an original   Woman   so
Nellie got caught ripping them off she did or didnt
who cares desperate cunt so her kid starts screaming
when he sees her couldnt shut him up so they took
him away to a better life her brain doesnt know
       move on to the next sad story i made

'The essential function of the universe,which is a
  machine for making gods.' —Henri Bergson

---

   as if Eternity sprawld in the bed,oblivious

---

    pimp her out into the vast spectatorship of night
nobodys watching but a vast eye,&it dreams in her
       absence,presence   all the same

Eva,the witch mannikin/womanskin inside glass dumb
girl on the bus public masturbators all of us aspects of
her furious beginnings,she sd imagine being told you
are too material   toExist   &there was Eva always
there the teutonic report to the oldgods she sd what
did you expect tear it up& begin again
                      dour &scribbling
       if there are Valkyries they were furies
  if there was Creation i am curious about its rationale
im another woman just onemore cagd here w/monsters
i imagind in original powers   cuz we luv the drama
as we multiplied into all these Others
    some creatures cant hear No w/out exploding

                      who are you

---

fatum < fari to speak < *bha* IndoEuropean root breath
      Fate occurs because we breathe   it was not
respectd

---

the discipline of night alone w/thought freaks you if
mortal if not   reminds   what you are

the only terrestrial animal who will fuck a corpse the
nova of extinction proliferates the stars w/orgasms of
corpses the only animal geard to exterminate his own
kind w/all the genius fire&ore&power at his disposal
which is Earth   to murder Life,the terms of his being
as if aVictory   you disagree prove me wrong

---

but he was there
but he was beautiful

    cut the deal
    cathedral   cathedral of his body architectd for some
    seeming glory   waitd weightd to appear meant
    solid,real

a pure description of night who has a body but it is
everywhere ultimate black spill from bones marrow
of stars into streets theyre made of the flesh of stars &
all his brilliant refusals

what did you want sd KnifeBoy i wuz the 1st Tool
in yr cosmic machinery

---

    if every joint was Chartres arthritic city staindglass
window of my last eye if every vein is a street to the
end yr body holy speeds thru tunnels of this architecture
invents a destination holy in this glassAtmosphere fixt
to break the crystal rigid w/age has become my last eye
the metals exhibitd in streets vials of heartbreak fluid
spill out of their mouths as time they say the taste of
oceans at end of a pier,is failure the wet spume drool of
stars you cant see anymore a mineral surrender to being
suckd there into so many mouths rust gangrene scum of
too much action the volcano of time a fireworks concludes
the night it falls thru plasms it was,originally a thought
so it was the transcendence of us white fluids lick my
eyelids forget the end beginning it ends it begins if every
nerve was a witness to torture fire it remembers a city
constructd of writhing fire
cut off their air see what their eyes scream jezus on the
cross or more air more air
joan cried out jezus jezus in the fire but as a pagan girl

gallic earth :god was her Lover thats all she knew
joan was a Fury fuckd betrayd by the boys game
move / on

there will be no more sea sd jezus good 4him the oceans
are blooming bloom swirling huge plastic flowers toxic
algae radiant metalife its a hot garden out there it glows
in the dark from space it glows eerie colors the suffocation
of air the face of gangrene smirks back at theMoon all
shiny &religious w/Death good4UjeezeUS all the bodies
rise up bloatd & rotten dead fish

leather jacket streetcorner needle in his brain or money
this is how we deal w/worlds weve made he sez its
nothing personal
        Balder the death of Balder murderd byFate ie
breathing (you did not read)

he liftd his ass in empty citylots to buy a fix no real
problem then pimping women a step up in bizness
spread yr cheeks &the old Greek spasmd his seasperm
into yr desert   deposits hiz jizm as into a bank &it
was his ancient poetry you did not read

belovd by all the story goes   if everything on earth wd
weep for him,every creature& plant,metals even metals
weep ,then he cd live   return to yr eyes   &Creation
does indeed weep for Baldr, all of grief(angr) except for
one   the hugeHag called Thokk hunchd in her cave
refuses
   Thokk will weep /   with dry tears
   for Baldr's journey to the pyre
   living or dead   / I have no joy of no man's son
   let Hell keep what she has
    & every substance does weep(METAL WEEPS, as
condensation consolation brought from ice intoFire)that
loves him   but the old giantess laxvulvad squatd in her
cave   refuses
   let Hel have him, no songs of man give me joy   the
beautiful boy the steel the iced iron brought into a warm
lifd place weeps its empathic sheen(always) the fire wants
him but alas(too bad)   the old hag in her cave says No
not a drop of sweat for him   shes all dried up,desertd
strewn w/rocks,hearthard   unmoist & *silm*   that lovely

moisture wept by the vulva   as moonlight on water
our sexd tears   is not
our memory of tears of course leak for Baldr but in her
cave i did not   for i must decide the end of worlds(she
thought)
      he goes toHel   was 1/2woman now all corpse
i am half woman half corpse   all the time

---

as magician i eat the brain thus enlarges powers a
brain of beast or human remembers in its meat (the)
wandering under stars for answers or curious things
unknown yet discoverd depositd a living memory it
can be eaten cannibalism of the planet who is thus
wizard thereby ruthless at expense of pain aDelirium
it feels all things &knows theSecret it is to feel All
Things and not beEstrangd to be Power but a willd
Explosion,nothing escapes enlargingOrbit of aMind
it squats alone in this cave carefully digests thoughts
of bear,poem of auroch,fear of this pain in his kind
why the teeth become sharp refind to a dogs wolfs
tooth designd to cut up meat &savor it the brains
are always soft yet something in them   listens,or
knows its mouth,enters w/out fear of this nextDeath
as imagination
                                              the
voracious Ma(w) yawning ginnungagap of abysmal
boredom(or ecstasy) of theGame as/if no thing
changes only theMachine advances
                        i am theMachine

_____*the goddessMoney*_____

Money was a goddess in Rome (not mine)

money ME *monere* < OFr < Lat *moneta*, mind, coinage,
funds < *Moneta*, epithet of Juno, temple of Juno at Rome
where money was made
Moneta a title given to 2 distinct goddesses:
1) the goddess of memory (identified w/Greek goddess
   Mnemosyne)
2) an epithet of Juno, called Juno Moneta (*Iuno Moneta*),

    epithet of Juno sisterwife of Iuppiter, Jove the King
    of Money
on CapitolineHill,in high Arx or citadel it overlooks the
RomanForum   *Templum Iunonis Monetae*
        the 1st conflation of mint w/Temple,official God
w/money ,as magisterial books,incontestable records of
historys acts stored securely also   as if forever
a stolid Temple of solid Rome wealth is forgd there,
coins,funds &accounts of memory etymology of money
the mythology of moneys memory
                      (strange runes i never read)
herTemple (not mine) where efficient gods are made

i am just a woman here,draggd a slave(perhaps) from
europe or simply a simple countryside i know i am
always used &dirty,like money bitten as hard coin or
eventually as paper rippd as passd around in numerous
&calculatd hands   coldcash as someday sd
                otherwise   possessing nothing,or
coins made of my metals   i prefer small stones,minerals
hard from the inside,as i am   multicolord& hard from
roadside dirt where i walkd   coins are harder to get
metals,manacles jewels for some
    a womans profile   hammerd on flesh

nam diva Monetas filia docuit 'since the divine daughter
of Moneta has taught...' sd Livius Andronicus (Odyssey,
Latin frag. 21) Junos epithet *Moneta* likely derives from
Greek moneres ('alone, unique') &/or Latin *monere* ('to
warn') as any protectress of funds warns of instability in
finance, or Fate asMemory alone &unique theMother of
Muses   she warns   /Barbara Walker, Women's
                                                Encyclopedia, 667/
alone,unique how strange a goddess of strict accounts
the goddess of Memory   to remind,warn or instruct &
what buys & sells builds,unbuilds more efficient than
Time ancient of obsolete gods

a mother i dont remember(Memory) it is amusing in a
brief life here as eros,the little Cupidity of gods dear
child ofLove as i might be,noone knows hangs around
the grimy banksteps sells itself us untaught& whorish
someday this will be aXtian church as popes sell mercy
the little amulets &holy medals blessd,traded for sins yr

flesh yr money rubbd in imperial fingers   watch gods
wear down   not us

what openspace grasspark is left a few sleep there benches
under trees a huge black man talks to a certain tree stands
hours before it palmtree merciless no water he babbles to
barebark trunk because this is daylight &heat lost people
rebecome crazy as original trees are gods these are swords
thru yr head sparce lifeblood dript down from highrise
                                              clouds rare & indifferent

he   i do not remember time
i think Eva is writing the history ofTime   she sits there
stonesteps outside moneys temple no toga or grace but
a dark jacket,trousers croppd hair dry &dead brown her
colors a dark bag dumpd on some holyplace of business
                    she writes   the Western
worlds invention of clocks Doomsday god as deadline
guillotine punishment for a lifespan begins & ends in
just a woman here or female version of a species
nothing known beyond the End of a life
some crime Ragnarok ends then begins again this
guillotine never ends its sudden fall /eclipse
                                                as
Money squats inside her Temple (not mine) memory
money moony on her throne   a MedievalGerman sect
ofCathari worshippd the moon asHeva(Eve) ,Mother of
All Living   1st version of a virgin   Mary
                                   or other lives
 i am some woman here or female version of a species
nothing ownd beyond the End of a life

he   he
must be a priest(here) his fastidious declensions
of which eyes are born to iridesce at the corner of
Nowhere to Now   he appears on the street and sex
lights up the female green eyes i want to confess its
compulsive theLust makes traffic move the fingers
enter holy water between yr thighs u luv it bitch he
articulates & yr eyes flashd orbit all around earth all
(wh)orisons are glorious melt into this let yr eyes
become all hiz colors
                    panchromatic sensitive to all colors
hes an artist he cant think he can draw good w/a knife

a *pica* the most beautiful (always) in the room hes
always alone so his only tears weep for him like an
Actor upclose to gods lens staring as a camera waits
for something something to click record visualize
why such a world performs
            around him,like
moons around worlds

he liftd his ass to the gods when required for all is
holy in desire &we ate shit & we ate fire   no it was
all sacred all pure impure chaos &purpose *ab origo*
we ate shit & we ate fire & we were each other in this
acid cauldron Fate arrangd derangd again again to be
new again
        but i am Money

---

there are billboards huge documents w/rippd paper
over centuries griffito pulchritude the lurid actresses
ofVenus &strutting around the plaza senate arena
holy killingfloor the selfcastratd ones theFix ofPower
in them   subordinating flesh(eros)of their origyn
             so
i am just a woman here   *a female thing*
i am not one of them but watch

            Rome
who conquerd barbaricEva it sd w/pious money she
writes it down squalid on Temple steps no one knows
where she goes to shit,sleep eat   she doesnt sweat
in the heat or speak in runed tongues   a procuress or
businesswoman *Iuno Monetas* keeps accounts a ledger
of poems might be what she writes i am unread she
is strange   as i am
         incognito things
& under bridges,broken roofs or like feral dogs beggars
drab by the roadside,some anonymous rock or dried up
animal weeds grow thru rubble of my fingers things
as unsould objects(who) crouch quietly &wait among
the stones every empire grows from minerals like us

& then the man is(who)throws words at a tree a lip foam
the only moisture left in a desert of dumb rocks &the tree
doesnt (seem to) answer a man lights cigarettes w/his

burning eyes & then its time to kill something, because
an idiot woman is singsonging about the world along a
path &she gets it,one use for a dumbrock her head returns
to the cosmos   a cosmic process apparently someones
got to do it & the tree wont   answer   everyday i watch
this popular drama dust accumulates on a screen has
not been cleand for centuries it makes the picture
                                                                    happen

i believe the universe   dreams
                             _____

the shining psychosis of the male animal,his eyes fixd
on the kill as lust of beauty   inhabits him   drives his
engines into God   the female tracks as food
             eat God   & me   he sd
a lost boy the most distant(always) in the room he is
quite alone   his only gaze transfixes him asActor so
upclose to gods blindeye stares,asks of aUniverse what
comes next someone   to shudder cry soliloquize   his
scriptd emptiness   *i am not here, lost boy*
i drift in other space around yr staring sleep ask why
such a Void performs
                                    the theater is empty
a nude skinnygirl(he is)shedding flesh as deep thought
eyes of smoke,jacketdsteelskin famousStar of night
                                                               loves
nothing until itExplodes &fall of particles is you /loves
ecstatic rubble ,noisymoans &surgeries of you   /loves
masturbatd precision better than you   *locate*   his
ubiquity or recurrence on a street straitd/streakd thru
eons   the magicians quicktrick of novaSex
                          2hands: *fuck &death*
on the wheel of yr throat   speed of nowhere
   in historys performance   there is no difference
                    watch me he sd
(he)as anorexd girl as priest, junkie, pimp nihilist fuck
master user of flesh   *he hates it*   as Plato in a republic
of waste the wastdland hood he wears Inquisitioner,all
in black of criminals(of)darkness   (he is)
  i am good at this he sez
              retchd in a vomitorium,ceramic bowls
or wood altars preying, on his knees, eating cunt the
gears of grinding it the motorcycle revvd up for dark

power,lightspeed whatever it takes to get out
(he is) the starvd woman(her)suckd out erasure of
pain   here   not in   his eyes but glass   a city of glass
he curls up to sleep in   fixd in/difference   (is)
everybodys a junkie he sd   the drug varies   we dont
as
       spectacular timeTraffickd things go by
         the terrific wheels dont know me
cockroaches the opportunists of night   vomitsinks&
garbagedumps   where they liquidate   &repudiate   all
my flesh
   never trust a junkie junkies cant Love everybodys
   a junkie from the origynal alchemicFix   fixd
of yr Sulphurs, of yr Moons &Suns   of quicksilver &
   salt & semen & glistening *silm*   all that derives
      this   hardend material   *world*
              from some gold
  1st lovd   as loves ornament   or exchange for It
               /otherwise
dispersd by amnesia   i drift (as)calculates his escape
smoothes me in his cool hands   as
      money the variable   coin of flesh
calculates   rubbing,smoothing shines me up between
shrewd fingers,he has cool hands for the ordeal of buy
&sell   *lewd illusion*
he   all he ever wantd   to escape(this)(Life)   we made
      now i am money   doesnt matter

  sink down in the dirt here,material a bed for a night

  sink down on the curb here,in dirt   beg for food
              sleep

---

the omnivorous consciousness of the Universe

fuck ME attested in pseudo Latin *fuccant* (they) fuck,
decipherd < the coded form gxddbov   or some thought
fluocan: original of fuck,means to *curse*; later applied to
act of sex
      as money   cd care less

deep in the brain,a filmic eye   retinal cells reactive on
exposure toLight   singular,he though one organ not 1/2

of a pair photosensitive as if a gelid heat singlepurposd
mindcontrolld primal clitoralpenal a thermostat where
i morphate ambience mood of the genitalia &how it
coils&moves reptilian to its fatal target 2things chemic
magnetic of cosmic dance as gambit   now he gets
greedy crazy bored w/it &Money is better any face
hammerd into money *get yrEarthass ready* or perhaps
pfluog to plow, 'as in a field'(OHG)or the wizardsbone
middlelongest finger *the cursing finger* as arm extendd
palm down it blights blinds blasts theMind &powers
rushd hot cold not sensual but surgd down yr tubes into
fixd molds all yr property numbers laws seminal fluids
flushd down to soild,sexd,variant of sad biographies
of spread despair,my accountd flesh
   who i make a god makes me a dead thing dead bed
dead fish,down to calculations on a dime her florid cunt
buys a room w/no view dialVision you get flowers on
a table tv closet full of shoes or some primevalAlley
where yr knife conducts its   *ritual busyness*

   or 'fuck' traced to IndoEuro root *peuk-=*'to prick'

   all down to the scrotal fist fixt fetally coild
all down to that little coin in the brain (penal,pineal)
      that deals   the world

that idea of Time,ice Space solitudes convergd in us
that thought of heat,our sense forgd together in massive
cauldrons of potential things impossible to separate out
desire purpose result all one drama of specific eggs&
faces&stones if it was brutal it was lust of real for what
a body meant all real illusory noble &ignoble gases as
rut of minerals,erotic &rot blood i inventd for colors&
yr hot appetite how cd you forget the purpose of the 1st
night

      _____*the sublimatio*_____

sleeping i was(Gudrun) curld up tight to Sigurd(love)
                                 (Short poem about Gudrun,
                                    v. 24 Larrington 185)

but i woke faroff alone& cold she found herself cold
swimming in her lovers blood

she awoke in a red bed floatd in blood or a thrashing
or whalewings severing in the thickening waters flaild
alive or screamd(of)darkness & all the turning gears of
the sea unsynchd,gnashing break each other like terrible
teeth in a rippd mouth &ceaseless pounded into a heart
deep oceanic motors   ,& great blood gouts from
    her mouth   renouncing it

whales that once sing darkness under the waters bed
eruptd in its black flood ichor all the Greek gods black
bloodlike fluid coursd thru veins as their singing urgd
urgent of a Life & deep enwaterd as spermaceti drives
upward into lamp oil perfume,industrial&cosmeticEpic
powers&purposes of light,of whalebone corsets cinchd
squeezd her ribs,guts so tight &tiny she couldnt breathe
deep enough to know think run away or stript from
monstrous concepts her animal body   *this is love*
          pound from it
another blood oil Timecompressd it also sings black
upward *o energy this wd be love* some well drilld of
our body delirious w/inventions all the beasts whirld
in my brain barbaric metallurgists inventors of stone
laboratories(dreamd of)factories like the sea tidalling
wondrous products &Powers *we are relentless* the
glistend *silm* sweatd on me &yr sperm cunt&mouth
did i sing oily documents photographic&runic cinema
as if pourd from me for the 1st time *as if possibly
original* beasts gaggd w/yr prick &my delirium we
are one energy as an ocean spermneedle fixd into all
my dramatic veins sleepwalkd fluidly thru a glorious
damage *i think i wantd i achievd* as druggd drunk a
history of me as dervishstick drilld to make fire some
diorama lit up as yr eyes 3dimensiond+Time life&
dead things wild exhibits &artful scenery as if,light
shines thru   things creatures the beasts are stuffd &
staring &other objects as ifNature arrangd to be real
as i am shapeshiftd on epic scenery projectd to be real
light through holes our holybodies constant changd
costumes acts centuries(viewd thru a slit,clit openshut
in yr camera the voyeur aperture of my distance i am
elsewhere until this moment dissolvd toNow)the spun

fathoms swallow memory *a sextape like a sextape*
suckd from our orifices we thought isLove is this
dissolving script of bodyparts light spewd thru spit
&its holy acids eating me i am crazy now as others
i am crazy naked dispersd matter indifferent to itself
as others our face form figures dissolve asFlesh falls
off in the acid sea or (sadistic)tortures of fire &we
dont know who we are consuming everything into
my mouth   *o m n i v o r o u s*
   swirld w/Eva in the waters we are beasts,giants
grotesque creatures all my aspects going in &out yr
mysterious maws cunts interior oceans continuous wet
passages ive been before inside me of suddenly a
dead & glistening body of a horrible sea   there is a
deep museum of debris ominously still on earths floor
waiting for it to drift down sink down our legends &
glassencasd bones where all old gods &monsters sink
to sleep but their eyes are awake like glowing lamps
glowering always in the (glowering) dark
   there is a chair on the sea floor the realm of Ran
theRavager she collects drownd people in her webby
hands 9 waves of daughters pour out &pull back in
as uncessant into her mouth the debris of corpses in
variously decomposd stages,pieces of civilizations a
lone wooden chair on oceanic floor a kitchen chair
15,000 feet down in the watery kitchen or dark throne
oaken carvd heavy a runed chair stark ruin of a room
interrogations conductd there   3 miles under the sea
stony & staring imprisond by the waters emptied of
further motion a volva sits in trance sea creatures pour
from her mouth transportd sunk here 1000s years before
she rode coldlands wrapt in thick animal skins,carvd
wooden cart thick oakd axels shuddering theIce spoke
prophetic words seerd ofIce theVolva carried in wagons
of Ice site to site on high platforms where i sit in utter
trance full of this abyssal foresight memory foul oceand
throat utterd trance once of theGods or giants orFatal
stories memorable of those who sink down thru fathoms
& terrors to my kitchen i collect drownd bodies in my
pallorous &black nets floatd bloatd black pieces of it
now too ancient to eat   & Eva is one orNellie or all
unnamed women succumbd to it as we have all eaten
eachothersflesh godflesh rotten putrid w/sad romantic
dreams i suck this down fathoms of throats swallowed

to a watery room 'unpredictable&malicious' they say
of Ran a rune world i stare out from satiate &not full
i believe this is true &after Love is Death *is true* &
no one will eat the corpsing matter spiralld down from
drownd history no one will eat the foul sad waters flown
from Evas historic body thats my job in the end(ofEva)
her offensive juices & secretive cuntworks taste of
batteryacid,sulfurics &other fuels that make things run
(move)here in directions far off or exploded close as
here everything here eating everything here swirld &
spread wide open for the last business junk maelstromd
as gods giants myths wizards priests engineers murder
an oily film i am eating,eaten cunt as dissolving fish
Eva Nellie what is yr name unknown because i know
how it feels the original slowspread warmth newWorld
orignyal heat of ourCreation suck his dick also his cold
fingers lick eyelids as if he cd live again all yr pure hurt
juices back into me girl on the bus i am doesnt know i
love her hurt girls Nellie the bitches lockd in glass/Eye
where is the camera are the cameras watching all such
suckh back into me thru their cunts my mouth inhales
the fumes &salt they breathe& secretd a million years
of bodies perfume stink expression of my body *&he
the girl knew how it felt fuck you fuck you we were
gods u pimp* eva nellie dumb lost girls haggard deities
women circling in vortex legs spread open pouring their
contributions into maelstrom galaxies may form from
them as in sewers we are born *u stupid star sweatd
out as silm from my cunt* she will notForget she always
forgets as Wolf &Snake or gods or giants forget as
requird before conception of its favorite nightmare
the rush is brilliant lethally known by inhabitants of a
planet again &again repeatd absorbd into moist dreams
the cinema unwinds the body morphs its seizures thru
all the stages of our starry Doom
 she stares into us a certain doom inside her eyes
as if fish swim in there

*& Sagar sees the fires the Eagles windwings boiling
them &old &powerless Rym the stormgod rudders
Naglfar who dreams to sail west into it hits the wall
Naglfar the ship i built w/dead mens fingernails &
relentless it sails itself thru the fatal water &Wolf
&Snake are my brothers riding also icy ships or wild*

howls of the soil or thunders which are deadmens stony
feet & when everything dies giants&gods die they all
die   i do not die   i am Hel
        i know this well

Worm maggots mother myself familiar in our corpse
eating aspect there is a saltsweet rotten taste as cunt
or jism rancid smeard on her uncountable mouths &of
a certain doom inside her eyes as if ancient fish swam
in there undersea in the parkinglot submergd *i am in*
a desert at the end of the world Eva her nameless
girls slouchd poets junkies we are not magic now as
the tide sluicd in&out our eyes desolves us alone in
a drowning desert at the end of a world & all are
actors here perform a living theater of theEnd slimed
mergers&acquisitions murders&inquisitions chemic
criminal assets acids from innocent origins ofDesire
behold us this is all our body sacrificial who will be
us our liquids mingld in alleys public toilets garbage
dumps soup of desperate gods we cannot escape this
dissolution into each others cess& then we are
                                       sublime
& forgotten   it begins again

---

radiant he made me radiant,electric or darkness as
  at the beginning   our Romance
sublimatio to enflesh the spirit to vaporize distill the
body & asIf One   become theOther   understood

he made me radiant(ate) *my ownNight   toxicLight*
he made me radiant in his veins transfixd by needles
this is sacred night orgy of transubstantiation scried
on screen or on this scream of emptied air yr gangsex
the brotherhood of fuck arrives the necessary pain
&of melting glass into.....cauldrons,skulls yr sacred
cup,the 1st womb,hideous blindness, gasping mouth
of creature
splayd on ocean bottom her gapd cunt
              relentless relentless my drunken brain
cant stop this   to pour us out

faino >Sanscrit bha 'to shine forth' 'to breathe' 'fate'
fari > Greek: to speak > fanein: to shine

cano >Latin: to sing &*candeo* >L: to shine >common
Sanscrit root(?): 'to shine forth'
fmz >Gr: 'a light' & 'man' in his prerogative of speech

to escape like some sublimating vapor,a smell of gas
in his wake sped up speeds off he the automatic mute
girl who hates it   the flesh because(he was) a girl
   once   always stuffd in his pants   the shy cunt
&humiliation of wanting it   *asIf not*   sublime,his

   or *fuck* <IE peuk-='to prick'(also expunge, impugn
poignant, pounce pugilist puncture punctuate pungent
pygmy) punk be a punk get punkd in the ass
boxd for bizness piece of,pkg of   get yr ass ready
                           fuckd
fuckd

enargeia: Greek 'bright' 'bright unbearable reality' the
word used when gods come to earth not in disguise but
as themselves *energy*

energy   it is the 1st god   as cruel as beautiful eruptd
fire in oceans light in veins of whales sperm thick oozd
in this head under pressure urgd to spout into/as radiant
light or in those days the cavernd walls murky w/beast
shapes who moved engineerd circles around me all
waiting weightd my eyes opening   wondrous
                                         druggd
because i pull the plug in the sea because i empty the
sky i dont know why except its over run out in the
litoral West rushd over the edge all the dioramic debris
of possible interventions exoventions his technofixt of
my body adrift in space   i seem to need this story
in extremis   *i perform catastrophe*   (that)
it happend again   the cosmic rerun that recurrent
in my brain like the sea

   unbearable   *Reality*

a Universe fucks gets drunk in all the animals is you
you are representational or a symbolic act Earth a
woman on a stage who strips down to nothing but the
final question who cares you think its a cosmic joke
after all mechanical things impact yr uterus ores or

other poetries extractd from words accumulatd bruises
and levels exspelld of ancient runes you know recall
from bottoms of the glass or

---

here are the runes
the Norns carved the runes   *Urd Verdandi Skuld*
every living thing knows what is what was what
will be   Fate Becoming Must-be
Become
Becoming
Shall Be
the world resounds the witch is flying

or air screams,or fathoms pound yr ears or any howl
of vortextd ruins   wherever it hovers or shrieks the
runes on woodchips *blotspann* i mark them sacrificd
blood,shaken tossd as dice yrFate 3signs chosen,cut
of nutbearing trrees *i have intention* the codes silicon
chips in yr eyes the stories on blood ships sent toEnd
theWorld dropt red scalding from cunts doomcells
neurond on the skull   solderd hammerd on boiling
silvery oceanic fix
                    *of fingernails scrapd raw the waters
thick w/them*
of plastoid   messages   all are very tired of
                                        screaming
            whales &the sea that brought us kelpt
saltd ravenous for this nude world a body so clean&
begun again
w/whales &all swirling inventions in oceans choking
as drownd in our elements
&our sex was oild and metalld from the 1st night
vectord to this shards of glass on the seafloor watery
mirrors fisheyes stare into & do not recognize us
& now gone
nor the great North & West barbaric metallurgists
inventors of stone laboratories alembics of futures
my favorite myths of desire&mentalic numbers as
scratchd on wood or lazerd in circuitd atmospheres
by my eye
these are the runes
there is a Shade who becomes them Shadow in my
memory sal a salt of ice&fire it was sweat of the1st

world   i was not ashamd

glacial Andean ice 1600years to form,meltd in 25
indigenous selves used seep oil for ointment insect
repellant skin coloring&religious ceremonies escapd
from earth in gas or liquid drilld 1859 for this fuel
 news of the world i print these daily black runes
questions,knowledges redundances we dont escape
no thing escapes not gods,fates who must proceed
as sd
we flicker back&forth specific names&beings
archetypes who are not personal
another enraptd in ice melting fast cd not utter fast
enough
drill the oceans death song of whales inkblack seas
suckd for whaleoil before earth or yr eyes as stained
glass reflects some glory blood i invented for colors&
heat that idea of heat of mentald light ofAlgorithmic
civilizations
all the technopowers of the gods as human energies
in final orgy smear over into darkness where they
may now
disappear   to sleep
   *this much do i know and more can tell all
   of the weird   of the gods*

we sink down we rise up this much do i know   i sd
Medusas black blood of murdered oceans born out of
it a beautiful horse   ride up/rise up
    Skinfaxi stallion of the daylight
    Hrimfaxi horse of night,bridle dript morning dew
there were Valkyries of wings like swans or imagind
horses we slowly rise & are not swervd or hurried of
purpose our arrival of/on majestic haunches into great
halls of gods and giants nonchangd of death or life
so belovd are both,compulsd majestically
                                 this occurs
in a skull so large   as unseen
& the horses deliver us   deliberate,as on wings
as day as night,Eva Nellie lift from the maelstrom
& swirld dust repeats   all is relentlessly done
      the streetcorner hag downtown Tucson $banks
      cafes Walgreens a scrawny fixture some shirt a
      skirt bare native legs tennies no socks clockwork

52   Barbara Mor   theVictory of sex &Metal

she turnd ass tiltd upward smackd it her tossd
up skirt flashing bare ass buttocks of a child a
nude hairless vulva her greetings from Tucson
to passing shoppers officeworkers tourist trade
snap her photo its a postcard from,*Valhalla*
Vindheim   home of the winds   is her flabby cunt
Nithhog circles her bony roots her spine is no tree
the desert is empty a reptile eats its traffickd metals
w/no stop   repeat repeat
    she rides the glorious horse who does not look
    back or bow its head its buttocks proud of itself
    and she is glorious
enactd bravely badly as assignd or dreamd as i will
write it all down   sd Eva   Nelly   Norns as we fly
to the Gate of(Death/Hel   *valhalla*   ) i amHel
&there is no difference
all consumes all   theMind   after all   hungers
      maggots: mathk, matha (mother)   there is
a reason to forget this sagas   redundance:
&they all die&then return Hels brothers the Fenris
wolf & Midgardserpent die(repeat)their sisterHell
does not   theNight is hers   relentlessly sleepless
&quiet[d]   solitude is hers,darkspace some stars

    welcome to Valhalla   show us yr scars

1980

yr in some junk bar laughing yr bracelets are ropes of
oil sex encircles the world as snakes umbilical & cool
life at the end of the world   youve been here before
this is history in the last age of demonstration of the
real
                indifferent on a stage of bored muscle black
eruptions of her dance she our porno mother elaborates
and executes a birth sleek in a void as silent agony of
tranced breath or slaughter noise heard on 1st assembly
line into cars&meat this night moves toward death it
moves thru you as twists in expensive chains yr flesh
hoodd eyes slide sideways on swivels of light imminent
glaciers clink in fingers against the holocausts of glass
and yr head is back *singing* teeth as a white precipice
the room slides forward over you on thick wheels
(these are victorious nights   it is the winners hour)

&thru all bodies underground tunnels where jobs are
done and rats eyes are bulbs in wire cages fatal cars
insects of stealth and gears move   urine civilizations
into the wounds of buildings exoskeletal bedrooms
deposit eggs of oil in the mouths of sleepers &cunts
of mothers giving birth in hall toilets(this is someones
luxury wombs of cracked porcelain hotel spasms of
businessmen shot thru gray drains)   biologic eons
flushd down vaginas rented by the night stench &
dollars transact your sex in swirling Lysol the clocks
hearts convulse this is absolute time coordinates of
organs planets far off &a pulse throbbd in yr throat
as if inevitable voyeurs watch death reproduce itself
cold level by level dismembered hands of buildings
light yr cigarettes w/ripped music rise and fall of
stained elevators thru yr bodys ecstasy &someone
enters solitude a closet to scrape sick juices from the
4 walls

so night moves down corridors arrangements of bodies
purses of bodies open sex drunk on money(sediments
of sleek thighs open options drilled by money)the baby
cries for milk vomits batteries &thin oil fugitive shoes
of a father run over its crib sheets used cockroaches of
radio words peel the walls dry music of used fingernails
sinister wallets underworld leathers stop beyond doors

(a mother bequeaths a last sensation raped by phallic
metal) chemical stairs dissolve the starving feet that
run from her mouth
                    this is someones vision of a life
    alleys move like snakes mafias w/belts of grease
cop pricks &gunned crowds explode jet eels on retinas
as slick magazines of yr skin open debouching money
a sexual woman spreading lipstick poison orgasming
bowels of metallic plates that gnaw &crash thru wet
massacres(this is the absolute hour this is death)thru
voluptuous tunnels erupting bodies the mother comes
dripping fetal oil(as blood)spreading out like skirts
as you rise to dance

this is a rite of the final night

                 ****

— drunk on it
— what i drink is Time
silence
— swung out over time its world convulsions
   slid between yr eyes and green breasts as
   animals slide in cages
   from cliffs of buildings into the sea
   bodies swing out over darkness on giant cranes
   in huge archaic arms
   sink as we fall from sleep to seas floor
   slower than we began
silence
— what is ragnarok you drunk bitch you cannot read
   yr own name scrawld red/read on the mirror in
   last allnite motel you stared yrself into
   what you think is yrs
— what i think is Time
— deathfucker
— silence

                 ****

theEnd: *it is not you it is her*

her cunt was oild metal and her mystery and her voice and
wings rising from swamp forests dripping scales of light
from her and the wind was oil and metal footprints

and highways huge skeletal shadows crawling thru black pitch
toward her name and the seas are oil
the dazzling rigs of cities of burst oil
her fingernails are steel and oil tides surge blackly
at the edges of her hands
her heart is oil sliding open in the dark like a warehouse
where trucks unload their black lines fossils
of endless cries

metalloid is her body turning in slick beds
among shells and repeated eyelids packed in silence
the bending of ferns and gestures of
enormous flight arm bones dripping with black gravity
oil is her breath fractioned from wreckyards from night pools
diatoms and bolts of insects on fire crushed inside her
the exhalations shine in windows on the beasts necks
twisted in rubble the roar
of oil rising in long elegant throats
erupting in black music jet heads
inside the flames whining and gnashing glassy foliage
her whispers in steel blades the hisses
of elevators jewels
of sweat drip from light glide as reptile shadows return
to original oil in the basements of eons body gears
grind into her liquid stations spider webs
corpse hands subterranean cables the telephone she uses
to call you into the last night

black rayon draped over nothing oil is her throat
and her eyes vinyl apertures the mood
falls into and spins in thin disks thru a dark machinery
small wires of insects suck from electric flowers
and the pistils are oil and green wounds of lawns
oil is her breasts and the childrens
black toys the fruits of the trees are oil the roots the seeds
radios of singing teeth that scatter them
nets thrown from her kitchen her linoleum thighs her deaths
sliding across retinas stab wounds
rapes interior mining where oil drips from her screaming
on the livingroom rug on bar stools on groins unzipped
in such exotic theaters

ink is oil ink hemorrhages from a mind
convulsed as earth by mute drilling the terror of

thought rushing to describe it
as her eyes rush to mirrors breaking inside
her oil is metals sleep
oozing from crevasses warm fur of animals flayed
in a vast silence large desks of men with
secrets stuffd in moist drawers children rotting on papers
a lipstick fire ignites their final empires her red lips
sluicing down metallic torsos
the sperm of executives thickens in quiet bays wild birds
struggle to rise cries choked on white graphs
final numbers oil is her tongues
plummeting like sirens at noon the black words
spreading over blank pages of sky
torn pages of water

she is oil in the supernatural engines the
dream of oil glistening on dull bones steel tanks thru
snow tracking solitary blood drops the woman with victorious
teeth advertising death traps and smiles
her long arm wraps around towns of ice her body cells
growing like a thick blanket as the mothers die
in agony the fathers die she covers them
as dinosaurs and ancient forests humus
from the bowels of tractors gray antennae cracking
fertile skulls of buildings
long shins cracked and sucked for their dark fuel
oil seeps thru veins conduits bedroom walls with stains
like bruises and inexorable birth she
covers them multiplying
children from a deep well the
slick air becomes them and the dead sea and spurts of
black milk entering the slippery mouths she gushes
generations who become her the pupils of
their eyes sleek and widening

****

there comes the dark dragon flying the
shining serpent up from Dark-of-moon Hills   (Voluspa last stanza v.66
Nidhogg flies over the plain in his wings   Larrington 13)
he carries corpses now she must sink down

****

there are nets in the eye that catch the light images
like wild beasts are gathered in tints of flesh
moving thru high grasses blades of helicopters rounding up
stray clouds a white horse
rears behind a chainlink fence a woman convulses
thru the thick eyelashes of death hidden cameras who capture
earth like prey angles of skin thrashing and
the steel neighing of the wind and bodies falling slowly
inward to the spread retina
as the drowned sink thru darkening lenses of the sea

skeins groping gathering what is done naked bodies
on ocean bottom wrapped in
baling wire blind maps powerlines coiled as serpents veins
of rabid dogs ancient fish swim by
growing gears and claws the brain
is drawing black lines around the faces of windows bored guns
stretch out calm along the sides of sharks
submarines sunk between tall buildings dinosaurs
in extinct shoulders of engineers stars what is left of
neon wedged in dark throats
shiny black lines stitch up anemones vulvas the sucking mouths
of the great crowd continents
wounded like beasts trailing bandages of water images
twist in the brain like
snapshots of caught fish trussed
with ropes of salt and imploding umbilical knots

mortises and scales of deep museums reptiles of
cold walls long echoes the weight of oceans on locked glass
cases of eyelids cracks in stone where horses
are leaping hooves thrashing out
nerve nets hang in underground rooms strung with pale tissue
wrenches of iron ganglia open their mouths
and the wind screams thru them tapestries evolve thru skulls
in peristaltic rolls the history of protoplasm
of surgery of mirrors lost civilizations with their skins
preserved around steel bowels calcium blueprints
in the tile of floors where
people danced ten thousand years below the sea

sunk in beds of gravity and black fire basalt
stitches flagellates and cities from
our still bones and bellies of spiders drift among the waters

with silent engines all nets are loosened
in a steady breathing
and tightened again and loosened again as photons and
worlds are woven and undone by
the retina as eons sink thru night
with its webbed hands

     ****

this much do i know
 & more can tell   All of the weird of the gods

Fuck you she heard
call of the wild levis blackjacket leaning on walls
hiz green heroin eyes black hair wind everybodys
teenage dream theNightmare waiting to happen it
waits leaning against aVoid slumpd in blackjackt
insomnia dreams you dream him

 iarp shwa(k)al rifna uk ubhimin
Viking rune depicting end of the world   i see
tattood on some strippd body,dead trucks license
rust gangwall he spit time on it was his secret
name to utter it is death
  Earth& Heaven will burst

    _____coda_____

some planets Knife Boy i do not know upon them
the acetylene light corrosions of 3 moons or no water
but something bleeds its components someday &
collisions of yr driftd molecules   maybe it will be
other worlds some day or us
— fuck you it sd
— sleep

— fuck you it sd
— gone

/ / the Victory of sex &Metal / /

/a retro metaphysical punk graffix in progress from 1981/
/ book #1 in a trilogy: Metals /
/ copyright Barbara Mor Spring 1991, Oct 19 2013
/ 1980 version excerpt in Sulfur 28, Spring 1991
ed Clayton Eshleman /

24/7 AND YR DREAMS
An Interview with Barbara Mor

by Adam Engel

1
Real Time, Real World

> What purported to be The Word of God was used as a ritual whip to sever Human Flesh and Spirit from its primal Context; the Human Mind thus forcibly separated from (con)sensual experience in the name of a disembodied Value. Generations were taught to fear and distrust "Nature"—redefined as a demon-inhabited, temptational Enemy.
> —Barbara Mor

ENGEL: Today, mathematics is the language used to describe all manner of natural events and phenomena, from quantum physics to chemistry and to a lesser extent biology (which is where modern medicine fails, because you can't quantify life with numbers, so they just throw chemistry at biology and hope the drugs work). But in "ancient times" the symbols of the Goddess (art, hieroglyphs, various markings and other forms of communication, e.g. cave paintings) were used to describe the same phenomena. And it worked as well as Mathematics. Are todays technologies, steeped in the language of mathematics, just variations of the technologies of the ancients, based on the languages of art, markings in stone, early writing, and music?

MOR: Consider Text/Context. For circa 45–50,000 years of preliterate homo-sapiens time on earth, our Human Text was the same as our Human

Context: The Natural World (once called the Real World). Seasons, regional weather and terrain, patterns of night sky, sun, moon, planets and stars, animal and plant cycles, the human lunar-based fertility cycle: This contextual world—which is all there was, 24/7, and yr dreams—was read as simultaneous pragmatic and sacred Text. Human technology grew via reciprocal interaction with a living world: Hands, sticks and rocks; a keenly observed environment; flora and fauna; it all became human culture: fire, cooking, clothing, fiber textiles, herbal medicines, hunting and habitat tools, art, music, language, ritual. Science began here, long before the written word; "science" was a continuous occurrence, daily life. And natural context was sacred text. World was The Book.

In Cro-Magnon cave art and carved bone items, we see not only a precise imaging of the natural world, rendered with esthetic skill, but we also see a tender love of this world. They were up against the awesome beginning, our human forebears, they survived the last Ice Age without central heating or TV weather news. We know they suffered (arthritis, toothache, broken bones, infection) and they knew death, short life spans. But nothing in their art shows cringing Terror, or ontologic hostility. Rather, they were At Home on this planet: A part of it, not apart from it. Context was Text, and these first human recorders were self-inscribed within it, not alien observers.

Time marches on. Once Time circled, now it marches. Tickticktick. What happened? John Zerzan ("Why Primitivism?" in ANARCHY, Fall/Winter 03-04) quotes Guy DeBord's biographer Anselm Jappe, who asked why "the results of human activity are so antagonistic to humanity"? Our definitive Angel, the human desire to Know, leads us into present Hell. The Force of Paradox is within us, and it sucks.

A useful book is Leonard Shlain's *The Alphabet Versus the Goddess: The Conflict Between Word and Image* (Penguin Arkana, 1998). The title mirrors yr question. Neolithic abundance, Bronze Age beginnings of "civilization," a context increasingly designed as a human power-space vis-a-vis Nature. Early writing (2500-3000 BCE) used for both sacred texts and clerical accounting around the royal granaries, empowering hierarchies, etc. We know the story: Ur, Sumer, Babylon, all those clay tablets, the first writing—all now compose the dust and rubble of Iraq.

The Abstraction of Writing, when It Became God, comes down to us as The Bible. The Abrahamic religions (Judaism, Christianity, Islam), despite chronic in-fighting, are One Religion, monotheistic and exclusive in intent, based on a Text that purports to be the Only True Word of God (Torah, Old and New Testaments, Koran). Embodied in a Book, this Sacred Text claims a God who is abstracted from all natural context, is indeed a Word

AGAINST the sensible World. That is, what Nature's World tells yr senses, Gods Word corrects, denies, defies, forbids, punishes beyond death. In any contradiction between the two, God as Text prevails over World as Context. In extreme Fundamentalist readings, they are at eternal war.

The taboos on Image/Image-making in Bible and Koran enforce this Turning Away from the credibility and reciprocity of Natures Text/Context. And from its primal power over our human consciousness. One can't make "images" of Nature—as our Cro-Magnon ancestors so brilliantly did—without touching Nature, intimately and fondly. The iconoclastic Biblical mandate to "break the Images" of surrounding pagan cultures was Gods ascetic word: Don t Touch.

This Loving Nature was commanded to Look Away from Itself (from our species sensual Context), away from Nature and Nature's Imagination into the Mental Abstractions of Gods (unillustrated) Word.

The portability of the Bible (a Text/Context detached from Nature) became a signature of Jewish endurance, continuity throughout Diaspora; so for Jews the Old Testament did perform both sacred and pragmatic functions. For other people, dissemination of the Bible was a disaster. Moving through Western history, it was used as a Power Tool, a weapon of conquest and colonization, from Imperial Rome through European hegemony, thence into the imperialized globe. What purported to be The Word of God was used as a ritual whip to sever Human Flesh and Spirit from its primal Context; the Human Mind thus forcibly separated from (con)sensual experience in the name of a disembodied Value. Generations were taught to fear and distrust "Nature"—redefined as a demon-inhabited, temptational Enemy. Only "The Word of God" could be trusted, but this Word derived from a textual context which rarely, if ever, applied to the supplicant. Forest people, mountain people, steppe, jungle, and sea people were confronted with a (fully-armed) Desert God, mandating morals and worldviews vastly disjunct from their pagan knowledge of their own experiential terrain. Such a disconnect makes people wacko, especially when it invokes Conversion by Fire, Sword and Cannon. (Or by Law and Money; the West's secular tools of persuasion derive from the same disconnect.)

Freud believed that the urgency of the Western search for scientific truth derived from the Biblical obsession with moral rules, law and justice. Eric L. Santner (in "Freuds Moses," in *SEXUATION*, ed. Renata Salecl, Duke U. Press, 2000) contrasts this "nomotropic obsession" with the "pagan cosmotheism" of pre-Biblical human time, in which "we find direct enjoyment of cosmic Eros, of deum siva naturam" (Spinoza, in fact). The monotheistic abstraction of the numinous into Legal Text over and against (human) Nature possesses, Santner claims, an "uncanny energy"—the power to distinguish between a True and a False God, via possession/ adherence to the Right Text (or disobedience to It). A disincarnate Law, presented as God, becomes the Only Sacred Text negotiating between human group and the (by Biblical definition) outcast context of Nature, now comprehended as "good" solely to the extent it is controlled/resisted by human beings.

Freud was right in this sense: A God abstracted from Nature becomes a Deified Text abstracted from Reified Context. This set the tone for the Baconian "Interrogation of Nature" (which occurred in uncanny coincidence with the Churchs Inquisition of Witches); even when science defied religion in Western history, scientists wielded the same superior whip over Dumb Matter as did the priests over Errant Flesh. That is, Attitude is All. Freud was wrong, however, if he assumed Western science as the only possible (or "serious") science. Pagan cultures worldwide practiced Science: Fire, cooking, textiles, ceramics; herbal medicine, obstetrics and surgery; mathematics, geometry, astronomy. From Anasazi solstice/eclipse stone circles to Megalithic observatories throughout Europe, preliterate and pre-Biblical people charted the sky; Mayans invented the Zero; the Chinese I Ching as a digital computer that defines and accesses Process was cognized by Leibniz as the original binary number system. And so forth. And did Freud forget the un-Torahed Greeks?

Science, the human acquisition of knowledge about Nature, is indigenous to our Species.

Within our Context, we construct our Text. The most "primitive" peoples, isolated in Brazilian or Indonesian jungles, know even as children more Scientific Data re the fauna and flora of their habitat than the average urban resident of any modern city. How such pagan sciences would or could develop into World Science we can't know: They were obliterated or co-opted within the colonizing Empire carrying the Power Tools of Law and God's Word, which rationalized the destruction/absorption of pagan knowledge into Imperial Booty as God's Will (a God who Conquers Nature, rather than Lives With Her).

So it is not a matter of Science: Yes or No. Science is Human Nature. It is the attitude with which science is pursued, and the ends it serves, matters that are under question.

Consider the American Indians "conquered" by Texts of the Invaders/ Colonizers: Bibles and Law, otherwise known as treaties with God, treaties with European royalty. Tens of thousands of years, mythic generations of epiphanal and practical interaction with the Context of this hemisphere (land, seasons, plants and animals, migration and cloud patterns, water streams and bird cries, the messages of insects and wind): Suddenly and totally Denied, countermanded and interrupted, overlaid with the surreal Unreal. An oral/aural people embodied within the World Around, they are handed these little paper rolls, pages of skin, scored with squiggly black marks that contain the Power, by any means necessary, to forever obliterate that original relationship: Nature herself brought to her knees, the primal Text/Context erased and replaced with a continent-sized "For Sale" sign. The natives were "ignorant," while "Western civilization" franchised the invaders. But which of them had the best Science?

Is "science" Plunder or Reciprocity? Time will tell. Tickticktick.

The Bible, Koran, any such Text purporting to be The Word of God, functions as a Code, a mind-program. Portable, indoctrinated generation by generation, it works to structure the brains perception of Context before that brain has a chance to experience Context in any other way. And as with any Code, it Replicates itself. That is, genes and memes. Just as DNA replicates biologically, the SacredPowerText replicates culturally. Thus the natural world is recreated, via programmed perception, in the image of a worldview, an ontological Code.

The forbiddance of Image/Image-making is a way to forbid any other program but This Text, which is a self-reinforcing system, a Cloning mechanism. This is what the Fundamentalist agendas do, they Clone believers. The Meme/Code is a loop between brain and world, and in the process both are reconfigured into an Unreality (a refusal of Nature) which yet has the Power to subvert the Real (our existence in Nature).

Not raised in any religion, I was introduced to the I Ching at age 13; it became my Text/Code.

I turned to it for answers and advice, as people turn to Bible or Koran. It did not, however, forbid other Texts upon pain of eternal damnation: Rather, it inculcated observation of process, without falling prey to Greed or Fear. Is this not a "scientific method"? Dating 1000-750 BCE, the I Ching easily inhabits the universe of quantum physics. Western science just got here.

Imagine two huge murals: One pictures war, bloody male wounds, mutilation and death; the other shows a woman giving birth, bloody orifices, membranes and life. The first is common in public spaces, the second taboo. The war scene is common in front page and television news;

the maternity scene isn't. Why? Our disembodied Value is killing us, yet we continue to worship It. Sex is profane, war is holy.

The Abrahamic Holy Men (Judaic, Christian, Muslim) more or less literally bang their heads, over and over, in the anguish of repetition, against their Wall of Text, monotheisms Idea of God's Word and Law—while all around them the Context of the World screams ENOUGH! Stop the delusional babble, the compulsive mumbling of beads, yr little turdstones of sacred alphabet. Yr God of Submissive Flesh is a continuous Lust for Pain—that is, yr Text wants to murder our Context. Observe what is being done to a Real Earth in the name and pursuit of a Dead Idea.

What brought us here is not Science, or Number, or Knowledge alone, but our ATTITUDE toward planetary embodiment, that is, Nature. We had a choice: Hostility, or affection. The Interrogation and Inquisition of a Witch. Or the fond curiosity felt toward a Lover. Our lethal science did not want to know Earth, but to escape Earth. But it is not Earth which is our Prison, but our Minds.

2
G.I. Jane

> In dysfunctional Western civilization (unemployment, class and race schisms, the necessity to maintain social control via positing of An Enemy), almost continuous war has provided the classic employment of Young Stud Energy, to the simultaneous double profit of Rich Older Men. Not only do the latter profit economically via war economies, that is, but sending off young men to distant wars leaves the Castles, Banks and Harems of the Homeland intact.
> —Barbara Mor

ENGEL: Someone sent me an article today about thirty-seven U.S. servicewomen who claim to have been raped by their fellow troops in Iraq and to have been "discouraged" by their superiors from complaining. So if thirty-seven came forward and were "discouraged," you gotta put the real number at ten times that amount. But the thing is, for me, by joining the U.S. Military, voluntarily, you are condoning the murder, rape and torture of tens of thousands of innocent, unarmed men, women and children—mostly women and children—across the planet. The women of Iraq did not join the U.S. Military voluntarily. The women of Iraq have no one to complain to, not even unsympathetic superiors, when American troops go on a rape/torture/murder spree. So the female troops of the U.S. Military are totally ignorant of all of this? Perhaps, because they were raped, 37 Iraqi women were spared. No one should be violated, ever. But can one compare suffering? The rape of a female soldier who knows war and weapons and violence, compared to the rape of an Iraqi housewife, who also knows war, weapons and violence, but only on the receiving end? All men and women should be fighting against the very idea of an American Military on missions of global conquest. Volunteering to join such a death machine puts you in the position of victimizer. Or at the very least, supporter of victimization. Should we feel bad for the victimizers who become victims themselves?

MOR: For the female soldiers raped by fellow troops, I feel the same sympathy, and for the same reasons, as I feel for all the soldiers, male and female, who end up killed or badly wounded. For whatever reason—kids wanting a shot at college, access to vocational training, a belief in the cause—they participate in the Mass Illusion of War as the defeat of Evil, the defense of God's Country, whatever. The more naive their illusion, the more painful its shattering will be.

Any culture's chronic problem is the employment of young male energy. Too much squirmy, unemployed testosterone threatens established order; mostly it threatens the older males in power with outright revolt, theft of their wealth, seduction of their women, etc. In dysfunctional Western civilization (unemployment, class and race schisms, the necessity to maintain social control via positing of An Enemy), almost continuous war has provided the classic employment of Young Stud Energy, to the simultaneous double profit of Rich Older Men. Not only do the latter profit economically via war economies, that is, but sending off young men to distant wars leaves the Castles, Banks and Harems of the Homeland intact. (Or, in patriarchal theory, it should do so.)

Young female energy, freed from traditional role-restraint, is also potent; if not engaged and patriotically directed, it can disrupt the Realm. The feminist egalitarian idea of Equal Rites involved opening the Armed Services to women; young women today are attracted to the same educational and vocational chances, and we offer these to low and middle income kids via the price of risking their lives. And/or, risking rape—from their own troops or from the enemy.

Warriorhood as proof of manhood is a cliché, but it rules. Because so many poor and ethnic males enter the armed forces to acquire the official Proof of Manhood Seal theyve been historically denied, they've resented entry of women and gays: if females and homosexuals can be Warriors too, there goes the social cachet power of the Military Uniform (and boot camp endured) as Proof of Manhood. Harassment of enlisted gays and women, including rape, is part of this revenge syndrome.

It would be cool, and helpful, if all this were openly discussed at the beginning of training; but it probably isn't. The military runs on the fuel of unquestioned Ideals; straight talk (including politically incorrect talk) subverts the gung-ho spirit.

That women can be warriors is not the issue. Ferocious female warriors are on record—in Africa, Asia, pre-Columbian America, from the Russian steppes across Europe into the British Isles: Women warriors are not new. In the past, however, they were tribal warriors, often leaders. And like Boudicca of the Iceni fighting against the Roman invasion of their homeland, they fought intensely defensive wars. Blood, soil, folkways, children: Up close and personal. Fighting for "American hegemony" is relatively abstract; I suspect some young women are gung-ho Barbies, trying to prove a patriotically-manufactured "womanhood." Certainly some female soldiers in Iraq and Afghanistan believe they are fighting for womens rights in those countries. The weird thing is, they wouldnt organize into an army of women to fight for female rights here in America: They think they're free enough, or if not, they depend on Big Daddy's System to give them what they need, when they've earned it, being Good Girls. As such, they fight for God and Country, and sometimes get raped. The radical question is: How many would fight for Earth and Country? And we know the answer: damn few.

3.
What's Left?

Man's Law, that is, which is always Right, is always in definitive control of Pain Distribution. The failure of the Left has always been its Fear of its own Dark Side. The "inchoate" Energies, described as Freudian Id, Jungian Unconscious, just general Funk and Fate, are the miasmic orgasms of the Female historically misnamed, misdiagnosed and bungled by the Good Doctors of social design. Western Patriarchy enters the Dark always in a missionary spirit, to "help" or "manage" or "cure" those parts of town assigned to crime, sex, poverty, intoxication, all the Transgressive Neighborhoods defined as problematic to the achievement of Paradise.

> The Artists and Poets know, or have known, that this Dark Turf exists primally, and exists Necessarily as urgent Medicine for a Sick Paradisial Ideal. It is not "the Dark" that needs help or cure, that is; rather: Doctor, Fix Yrself.
> —Barbara Mor

> Eschewing the Dark Side, the Left has no Vision. Left politics are mostly reactive, rarely creative. In Europe, for example, in opposition to the American-Israeli alliance of holy contempt for the world, the Left moves to embrace the Muslim cause—the Palestinians, yes, but also the French Muslim fundamentalist campaign to retain girls headscarves in the public schools. "The enemy of my enemy is my friend," sez the Leftie, and even goes so far as to believe this constitutes a chic, radical position. It is not radical but merely reactive. It establishes no principle or position, but merely a formula of alliances. Here is the place to quote that epigraph from Thoreau: "There are a thousand hacking at the branches of evil to one who is striking at the root."
> —Barbara Mor

> The Root of America is that it was once pagan, wild and various. Jefferson, Madison and Franklin, Marx and Engels learned from American Indians, not the reverse. Despite the Holy Liars, our Constitution is not "based on the Judeo-Christian Bible" but on the Iroquois Confederacy, with help from pagan European tribal systems, the Magna Carta, John Stuart Mill and Voltaire. To be reminded of this, Leftists should reread Thomas Paine, and revisit Thomas Morton and his Maypole. (Plus check out Jim Goad's The Redneck Manifesto.)
> —Barbara Mor

ENGEL: What's Left? (Who's Left is also implied, not to mention Sam Smith's classic, "Why Bother?")[3]

MOR: What's Left, literally, is The Sinister: the Body's Left Side (Dark Side of the Mother, the Flesh and the Heart): the Nagual. This is the realm that hyper-rational males from all points of the ideological spectrum have Dexterously (righteously) marked off as profane, errant, forbidden; or have worked to subordinate to some auxiliary category (Index under Politics and Women). The patriarchal mind, from Bible to Bacon, Marx to Freud, Bookchin to—yes, sorry—Nader, does not escape its Inquisitional fascination with strict daylight dogmatism, which quickly collapses into

---

[3] *Why Bother? Getting a Life in a Locked-down Land* (Feral House, 2001).

anal-obsessiveness over correct practice and procedure, ritual observance, the absolute length of beard-hair or number of whip-strokes per minute per breath of Crime: The exact size, shape, and weight of stones collected fervidly to be used to stone the radical body to its Deserved Death.

Man's Law, that is, which is always Right, is always in definitive control of Pain Distribution. The failure of the Left has always been its Fear of its own Dark Side. The "inchoate" Energies, described as Freudian Id, Jungian Unconscious, just general Funk and Fate, are the miasmic orgasms of the Female historically misnamed, misdiagnosed and bungled by the Good Doctors of social design. Western Patriarchy enters the Dark always in a missionary spirit, to "help" or "manage" or "cure" those parts of town assigned to crime, sex, poverty, intoxication, all the Transgressive Neighborhoods defined as problematic to the achievement of Paradise.

The Artists and Poets know, or have known, that this Dark Turf exists primally, and exists Necessarily as urgent Medicine for a Sick Paradisial Ideal. It is not "the Dark" that needs help or cure, that is; rather: Doctor, Fix Yrself.

Think of a Tapestry: perfect clarity on the daylight side, as disciplined threads appear to compose the picture. Turn it over, however, and you see what *makes* the picture: the strings of creation as crazy Technicolor snakes squirming, twisting, intercoursing around the terrain of the darkside. The power of Biology grows from Inside Darkness; the Seed and the Brain express their Interior Dark; six billion years of Earth manifested gorgeously before the Human Eye. This is the Mad Method which performs the Illusion of the Composition, and it Performs on and of the Dark Side.

The Side of Light functions righteously to Control and Commodify this primal reality. The historic "Left" has always used Female Energy to fuel its "Revolutions": Against the Father, the Church, the State. French women started the bread riots, stormed the Bastille, killed and were killed; victorious, however, their brothers-in-arms wrote laws to return French women to their skirts and their kitchens, and legally took away their guns, lest "feminine and domestic charms" be threatened by "empowerment." It's an old story. For example, todays Left disdains a politics of "population control," arguing correctly that it is the Industrialized West, of low population growth, which consumes a huge majority of earth's resources and exudes a huge percentage of earth's pollution. Ignoring, or dismissing, the fact that "population control" is a major factor and function of Female Liberation from our traditional abuse as cultural breed cows. Without female sexual autonomy, fascism is inevitable: the control of the female reproductive body by the male state is the Origin of Fascism.

But "women's issues" define, for Leftist males, subordinate issues. Ralph Nader tells us once again: "There is no difference between Democrats and Republicans." No woman in desperate need of an abortion would say that; Nader will never of course be in this or any other desperate need; and the next time he mouths this priestly drivel I hope a flock of grrrl crows and vultures attacks him and aborts his fetal words. I hope some tough and fertile bitch jumps up on stage and Punches Out His Lights.

Because this is all that's usefully Left: Bar sinister: Sons of the Lawless Side Bat sinister: Feral, crazy bat daughters.

Eschewing the Dark Side, the Left has no Vision. Left politics are mostly reactive, rarely creative. In Europe, for example, in opposition to the American-Israeli alliance of holy contempt for the world, the Left moves to embrace the Muslim cause—the Palestinians, yes, but also the French Muslim fundamentalist campaign to retain girls headscarves in the public schools. "The enemy of my enemy is my friend," sez the Leftie, and even goes so far as to believe this constitutes a chic, radical position. It is not radical but merely reactive. It establishes no principle or position, but merely a formula of alliances. Here is the place to quote that epigraph from Thoreau: "There are a thousand hacking at the branches of evil to one who is striking at the root."

Theres really no time left for any act but a strike at the Root, but most hackers on the Left have no clue as to its location.

Last year I saw a front page news photo showing an Israeli teen and her brother walking behind a Palestinian girl: The Israeli girl is reaching out to yank off the Muslim girl's headscarf. Its an act of religious and political harassment, yes. I despise Israel's behavior; I despise the American-Israeli collusion against the world; even so, looking at that photo, I have the same impulse as that Israeli teen. It's not a Jewish vs. Muslim impulse—I'm Irish Pagan—it is the Fist of the New against the Old, the Naked Mind against the Uniform, most of all the ShitKicking Reichian West against the Puritanic Repressive Religions. It is Knowledge versus Fear. Europe worked 500 years to crawl out of the God-Pit of the Inquisition, Europeans and the globally colonized have suffered millennia of religious, bible-based persecution and sectarian warfare, American women are still involved in essential struggle against "God" for autonomy of our bodies and our brains: This is the Root position. We must refuse to be dragged backward into that abyss. If Muslim women want to enjoy the relative "freedoms" of the West, they must know these freedoms are hard won, and always fragile. If you fear being "debauched by modernity," go home to the desert.

Women in burqas whose men carry rocket launchers is more than a surreal anachronism: it is the utmost in spiritual and intellectual hypocrisy. (A PoMo thesis that "the Enlightenment led to Auschwitz" by undermining the Western belief in "God" is equally fraudulent; that is, what then led to the pre-Enlightenment, "God-ordained" Inquisition, all 500 sadistic years of it? The Enlightenment was Europe's attempt to overcome the Inquisition: To the extent it failed we got the 20th-century Hells-on-Earth; to the extent it succeeded, we got us.)

The Left, long contemptuous of "religion," ineptly confronts the giant psychophysical social surges and erotic convulsions of Jihad and Holy War. Liberals and Leftists are afraid to confront "God"—except with the dry disdain that characterizes believers in secular rather than metaphysical Solutions. Turning chickenshit into formula, PC became a strategy for avoiding Root confrontation: a way to parade as Radical while not "offending" anyone.

A generation of earnest young politicos was educated to think you can solve a problem by correctly labeling it: Thats racist! Thats sexist! Thats religiously intolerant!

Well yeh, duh, so what else is *at the root*?

Christian America, Zionist Israel and the Muslim Fundamentalist regimes together are The 4th Reich; these bulldozer bullies for "God" will happily flatten every contradiction into rubble and upon this bloody plot build tacky Theme Parks of Pious Democrazy in the place of indigenous sensual global variety; these actual snuff games are being played out before our eyes and we do not accurately name them, or holistically denounce them, lest we Hurt Someone's Feelings—that is, everyone involved is a Victim of Historic Hurt, ergo beyond Critique. Mel Gibson's sacred S/M flick, *The Passion of the Christ,* appears right now to remind us that the biblical religions, all three, are based on the sadistic manipulation of guilt: You disobeyed God, You are Sinful, You killed Jesus, You are Filth and Dust Born of Woman, " yaddayaddayadda," the continuous manipulation of ontological *guilt* for the ontological *fact* of Being Alive on Earth. The Left does not usefully exist unless it denies/defies this Bizness of Guilt and embraces the Poetry of this Fact. But to do so, the Left must become open to the suffusion of FemaleErotic Darkness (which is The Female Mind) to a degree it has never accepted, insofar as the male-determined Left is in itself a familial disciple of that same Guilt-Trip Bizness.

Thus the Left has managed to turn off the world, revealing itself systemically as the DreamKillCopTwin of the tyrant Right. This rabid Right "frames the

Big Picture." For example, OReilly and Savage analogize 1) "The Anarchy on Our Borders, immigrants swamping our culture and sucking off our welfare" with 2) "Anarchy in Our Morality, gay rights, abortion, media hedonism, bastard babies sucking on Janet's exposed tit—they can do this because, being breathtakingly simple-minded, they construct without compunction simpleminded Pictures. (That is, blaming these "anarchies" on Liberalism, when every issue depicted is a function of cutthroat capitalist systems, re-employers seeking low-wage labor and media seeking profits, as mere human beings struggle and drown in the resultant floods of dislocation.) The Left can't frame "a Big Picture," or finds "a Big Picture" too Scary. It is unable or not willing to Challenge GOD, the BibleBoys, Yahweh Moses Jesus and Allah with their combined global BankAccounts. Leftist discourse has never addressed Religion as a power equal to Economics in the movement of human beings: the movement of passions as well as massed bodies. Only a witchy few second-wave feminists, a few brave citizens mounting First Amendment law suits, have stood up on their revolutionary hind legs to refute the TV preachers and radio bigmouths on their own turf, that is, Faux Holy Ground. These God Salesmen, in the bizness of vampirizing our human energies for 2000 years, can rely on Liberal Fear and Leftist Discomfort to join in avoidance of ontological battle over "sacred things: Who defines them?" Liberals pander, Leftists shrug and run. Meanwhile, next time a state judge installs his customized ten-ton version of the Biblical Ten Commandments in the middle of yr downtown courthouse, here's the argument: The First Amendment precludes the government from the establishment of a religion. The First Commandment is: "I am the Lord thy God, thou shalt have no other gods before me." And that is the establishment of a specific religion: An exclusive monotheism. The First Commandment directly contradicts and countermands the First Amendment. So every politician should be publicly challenged to choose between them: Yr Constitution or yr Bible? They can't: both rule this country. Europe, unlike America, has been the arena of historic disembowelment over issues of Holy War, Roman invasion and forced conversion of pagan tribes, Crusades and Inquisitions, the Catholic-Protestant mutual massacres called sectarian war, plus World War One, World War Two, Nazi death camps and Stalinist gulags, all "secular" extensions of the original FanaticVision. Europe is tired of it, we hope, and thereby wiser. Americans must look harder to find an authentic political position (the Archimedean leverage point) outside the mechanical Left-Right dualisms which decorate and twist our Trees dialectic branches but are not The Root. The Root of America is that it was once pagan, wild and various. Jefferson, Madison and Franklin, Marx and Engels learned from American Indians, not the reverse. Despite the Holy Liars, our Constitution is not "based on the Judeo-Christian Bible" but on the Iroquois Confederacy, with help from pagan European tribal systems, the Magna Carta, John Stuart Mill and Voltaire. To be reminded of this, Leftists should reread Thomas Paine, and revisit Thomas Morton and his Maypole. (Plus check out Jim Goad's *The Redneck Manifesto*.)

One European friend and intellectual comrade to Paine was Mary Wollstonecraft. Ring any bells? The Leftist dismissal of "women's issues" as secondary forces of change has robbed us of a potent(ial) Holism of Energies vis-a-vis the extant networks of Oppression: Church, State, Economic systems. Those feminists who attacked Patriarchy were not simply being "women" (that is, complainants within the system), but expressers of a bloody Outside Position: outside Taliban and Al Qaeda, outside Israel and Palestine, outside America and Israel, Outside the Holy War, which by definition is waged by and for the glory of the Hole-Stuffing Male, whose claims of GodHead subordinate all Nature and natural life and death to this WhollyDelusion: MonoTextandGun. Before being brainwashed into HandMaidens, all females are Born Rebels. Females are the Original Left, and it would've been nice to acknowledge this, and to grow upon this primal ground the alliance of Earth, Women, Children, Animals, Air Water Seed and Imagination *against* the Agony of Abrahamic Alienation.

4
Clitorally

> It is impossible to look through microscope or telescope and conclude Life is Absurd. Life works. The abstracted "mind" is absurd. Seasons, music, children, lizards, penguins, dung beetles: Life is not a Mistake. The sadistic emptying out of meaningfulness is the mistake. The Absurd is never a primal condition, but a stage of reaction: ones encounter with The Wall. The factory system, the prison cell, the torture chamber, the firing squad, the monthly rent, the morning commute, the quarter you dont have that must be dropped in the phone slot before you can call the governor to stop yr execution because you just dropped that coin in the toilet slot so you could sit and shit. What does any of this have to do with Life on planet Earth? Nature evolves biologic functions so it can exist in material form, but what Punishes those functions is human Idea.
> —Barbara Mor

ENGEL: While nature makes mistakes all the time, it never creates something for a purpose other than to sustain survival. *Except* for the clitoris, which exists for one reason and one reason only: To give women pleasure. What if the whole "harem" thing with a male having a harem of 100 females was an absolute perversion of what *really* should be going on? After all, that's one guy, with all his potential genetic flaws as well as goodies passing the same thing on to 100 other people and their children. What if it is the female who is supposed to have multiple lovers during her sexual lifetime?

Wouldn't it make more sense both ecologically, in terms of population, food, etc., and in terms of genetics, for one woman to have several children by different men than for 100 women to have children by one man so all his good and bad genes are repeated as opposed to a variety of gene "cocktails" resulting in say, five or six healthy offspring per woman? Variety of genes and ecology of population. Are we living in an upside-down world?

MOR: Imagine the entire Cosmos as a Gigantic Clitoris. No, seriously. The entire Universe is the erotic imagination materialized: Her Hologram. Orgasm is confirmation that Life Enjoys Itself. (If the puritanic/punitive god was our actual creator, sex would be total compulsion, but hideously painful: Think about it).

Beyond the human clitoris existent sui generis "for pleasure" (and its larger pragmatic version, the penis), the entire Universe exists for the "pleasure" of Itself: Chaos, novae, galactic bodies, stars, planets, fractals, flowers, frogs—that is Our Life In Art. Why? "After all," said Rimbaud, "Nature can be bored."

Given Infinite Time and Eternal Space—given capacity for Infinite and Eternal Boredom—what would you do? Invent! Ex nihilo, that black womb, conceiving string by quark by electron by cell by dream, what we call Evolution, or "Passing Time." The Fantasizer participates in all particles of the Embodied Fantasy, its Codes and Surprises, thus the signature of an electromagnetic erotic ecstasis appears throughout the Spectrum, micro to macro, just as Reich observed (knew). Einstein, in his major error, denied Quantum Theory because "God does not play dice with the Universe." God, as Female, does play dice with Herself, that is, is not a Mechanic standing outside His Machine, but is rather a Being Imagining/Evolving More Being. It is a Living Creation, pregnant with Risk of the Unknown, with all points in motion (friction) magically and perilously contingent upon all other moving points (frisson). Beyond Pleasure, that is, its about being Alive, which involves a cognizance that all else is, of the same being, Alive.

The human clitoris—never a problem before!—becomes fiendishly problematic for Patriarchal/Biblical religion, insofar as its existence confronts that religion with all of the above. If the Clitoris IS, that is, Yahweh isn't; or rather, man's Idea of God as defined in the Old Testicularment is confronted *a priori* with a better idea, the Real World, which posits not only female sensual autonomy but Female Choice as the mechanism/ determinant of evolutionary selection. The male whose genes are reproduced is the male who most pleases the female sensorium: Her eye, her ear, her touch, her olfactory palate. Bronze Age males who maneuvered to become Managers of Breeding (human as well as cattle), had first to deny this Female Primacy of Selection, redefining it as a Male Choice, "by God." Woman was reengineered from a sensual being into a livestock commodity, bred to reproduce male society in general, the husband's wealth in particular. Matrimonial sex, confined to reproduction, was understood at best as a Duty to God, at worst a Punishment for the Sin of Flesh; all other sex condemned to death by stoning. Needless to say, within these terms, the Clitoris became An Outlaw. It refuted the basic premise of patriarchal society: That Nature exists to enhance Man and will be disciplined or forced to do so in the Name of God. The denial and repression of clitoral knowledge that followed, that is Western History, not only made Life miserable for woman, with the impreached idea that she deserved lifelong misery as her existential definition; it also launched upon the natural world an orgiastic reactive violence, no doubt felt as condign punishment for Life's existence as dumb, yet seductive, matter: Earth, just like a Woman, deserves chronic fucking over for the crime of "objective" Being There. "She made me do it." "She asked for it." A thing that exists solely to be fucked, of course, elicits contempt. A woman who comes alive to enjoy fucking, under patriarchy, elicits death by rocks or fire (or fist or whatever). The entire S/M enterprise is erected upon the Biblical premise: She Can't Win. We live—and are dying—with the cosmologic ramifications of this premise.

It is impossible to look through microscope or telescope and conclude Life is Absurd. Life works. The abstracted "mind" is absurd. Seasons, music, children, lizards, penguins, dung beetles: Life is not a Mistake. The sadistic emptying out of meaningfulness is the mistake. The Absurd is never a primal condition, but a stage of reaction: one's encounter with The Wall. The factory system, the prison cell, the torture chamber, the firing squad, the monthly rent, the morning commute, the quarter you don't have that must be dropped in the phone slot before you can call the governor to stop yr execution because you just dropped that coin in the toilet slot so you could sit and shit. What does any of this have to do with Life on planet Earth? Nature evolves biologic functions so it can exist in material form, but what Punishes those functions is human Idea. Kafka doesn't describe "Life," after all, but the tortured creature trapped inside its mental constructs and devices, all originally intended to put "Life" in order. As if it could not be trusted to have its own Order. Or as if its own Order had been declared "demonic." Hostile to God and the bottom line. The plot to defame Matter as Dumb Mechanism, or Evil, lucrative as it has been for the bizness of Religion (and the religion of Busyness), now boomerangs against us because—oops!—Life R Us. Recall the Victorian practice of fastening sharp-barbed gloves on the hands of children and youth (and "crazy" adults) so that masturbation, if not stopped, would really, really hurt. Biblical religions invent and mandate these sadistic mittens. Capitalism manufactures and markets them. For Life to so hate and fear Itself, to the point of commodifying mutual mass systemic infliction of extreme pain, terror and degradation—nukes, landmines, cluster bombs, biochemical weapons, brothels, child sex traffic, refugee camps, famine, junk food, junk art, junk dreams—argues a powerful spasmic Interruption of Life's own ontological experience of Itself. We are not "cursed" by Life, Life is cursed by us. All Nature emptied of chthonic meaning, we now own that emptiness. And it really Hurts.

Monoism now rules the tonal (David Bohm's Explicate Order) with its replicable formulae: Monotheism monoculture monolithic monogamy monotony. The nagual (Implicate Order) goes on dreaming the Dark. The variants you describe—females with multiple sex partners, variety of genes and ecology of population—as well as a species dedicated to pleasure—exist now in sci-fi/fantasy (Ursula LeGuin in particular) and some quaint anthropology texts. We can imagine the arrangements of ancient Crete, matrifocal and pleasure-dedicated. Of course, the elites of all cultures manage to do their things: incestual, bisexual, polymorphously fickle, while they hire good nannies to raise the kids. They party every which way while keeping the plebs in straight line: for food, for sex and shelter, for citizenship, for God. Females are capable of vast polyrelationships. Patriarchal men are uptight, indoctrinated with Life's Possession (not its Enjoyment) as Proof of Manhood. But Earth is older than Patriarchy. And men are simply our most dysfunctional sisters (all males being half female, XY). The taboo on sexual polyforms derives from patriarchy's desperate need to keep everyone in Uniform, defined by gender, class, race, belief, etc. The fluid continuum of relational behaviors of which our species is capable (think Bonobo) would, if not ritually repressed, explode the current systems of Order and flood the planet with new (and ancient) arrangements. Males would be liberated, as much as females, by this genital revolution. The nagual, of course, is terrifying. Releasing people from bondage does not free them if their minds are still chained by bad ideas. Serial rapists, child rapists, sexual torturers, merchandisers: A growing population. Thanks to God and Capital, in the 20th and 21st centuries, the Bomb is bigger than the Clitoris: it gives Man the erotic power of Death, over all the planets trapped bodies. Does the average civilized male get more erotic charge out of a bomb than a clitoris? Yes. Making a woman come is no big deal. The Big Thrill is making her body explode, literally. Making any body explode literally. Yr biggest, and last, earth orgasm: And was it good for you? The mad bomber, like the rapist, becomes God, just like that. What we once called "pleasure" is quite perverted in the service of Power, and what can simply naked Nature do against mass pop PornoTech? The point is, Diversity is the Health of Nature. Monotony is Natures Death. The idea that terrestrial plurality (the Earth's Imagination) can be colonized and harnessed into a puritan global factory system, denies the monstrous power of the nagual to rebut constraint. It will explode, it will implode: It will not endure Monotony. Not for long. When it blows, we are the slick red petals of the explosion. When it implodes, we are the coal crushed to mad diamonds in the skull.

5
True Minds

> Patriarchal marriage depends on female virginity 1) to guarantee paternity of offspring, and 2) to guarantee wifely ignorance of any sex style other than her husbands. That is, her ignorance is his bliss: She has no comparative tool (so to speak). Female knowledge of sexuality, specifically our own, is the major Judeo-Christian-Islamic taboo: The female, not Dumb by Nature, must be made so by Law. Further, the female, not helpless by Nature, must be made dependent by Law. Marriage exists via the legal, religious and economic non-existence of women. This is why 19th century women were so brave to defy the institution, their extramarital choices being spinsterhood, poverty unto death, and/or prostitution. Women always worked; medieval guilds included female artisans (until the Inquisition listed them as heretical); but women's entry into the late 19th and 20th century workforce was revolutionary: With a paycheck, they no longer had to marry to survive.
> —Barbara Mor

ENGEL: Marriage is supposed to be about property and legal rights, but people seem to need it for other reasons as well. The recent attempts of gay and lesbian couples to marry are rooted in something deeper than who owns what. Marriage, whether religious or civil, seems to confer a legitimacy upon a relationship that "just living together," for no matter how long, does not.

MOR: My marriage skills equate my cooking skills (people who know me are laughing hysterically in Hell at this question)—and that is Zip.

I believe in Mating, and Relationships; Western patriarchal marriage as the monolithic norm of social organization is the problem. John Borneman and Laurie Kain Hart, authors of the *Washington Post* essay, are anthropologists. Anthropology shows us that marriage systems, like all human systems, emerge first as psychobioregional responses: people develop what they need for maximum survival and hope of flourishment within a given terrain, climate, economy of plant, animal and other natural resources. We are first an extended family, or matrifocal clan; then a tribe; then several tribes. Relations are one-on-one, and that between biological parents is rarely the most important: A stable context for the growth and education of the young, as Borneman and Hart describe, is primary, and its been achieved in many creative and wise ways throughout human history, none of them called "the nuclear family."

Religious and cultural Imperialism—the imposition, via guns and Bible, of One Way upon converts and colonies, despite Variant Reality—has been a disaster, and has succeeded because of the disaster: Destroyed indigenous networks, demoralization and self-alienation by foreign rules and ideas, enslavement or exile of the soul and body within a once native context now redefined as occupied territory. "Marriage," in this scenario, has functioned among American Indians, African slaves, Third World colonies in the same way it functioned among the pagan European tribes: As a tool of state regulation, thence inculcated into self-restriction and mutual oppression.

As for the Nukular Family, I view it through a 19th and 20th century radical feminist lens. Patriarchal marriage depends on female virginity 1) to guarantee paternity of offspring, and 2) to guarantee wifely ignorance of any sex style other than her husband's. That is, her ignorance is his bliss: She has no comparative tool (so to speak). Female knowledge of sexuality, specifically our own, is the major Judeo-Christian-Islamic taboo: The female, not Dumb by Nature, must be made so by Law. Further, the female, not helpless by Nature, must be made dependent by Law. Marriage exists via the legal, religious and economic non-existence of women. This is why 19th century women were so brave to defy the institution, their extramarital choices being spinsterhood, poverty unto death, and/ or prostitution. Women always worked; medieval guilds included female artisans (until the Inquisition listed them as heretical); but women's entry into the late 19th and 20th century workforce was revolutionary: With a paycheck, they no longer had to marry to survive. Women and men entering marriage voluntarily, rather than by coercion, should enhance the institution; if not, some people blame "Western freedom," while others question the institution. (Gay marriage performs the same challenge as feminism: We reject patriarchy's urge to control us via its clutch on our genitals.)

The Cleaver/Brady suburban cartoon norm called "family life" we all know exists to sell detergent and cereal boxes. The "nuclear family" is a 20th century invention, really a post-World War Two phenomenon, that came into being out of the need to build a peacetime economy out of home appliances and automobiles; before that, two adults were rarely alone inside four tight walls with their progeny and piles of debt; rather, they were surrounded by extended family, many hands to help in housework and in fields, women and men engaged in hard labor dignified by their mutual respect and respect for the earth (a respect that had survival value). Extended families, akin to tribal life, were the basis of American society; the modern marriage "breakdown" has not come via "female freedom," but via the condensation of this clan model into isolated two-parent households, far from built-in networks of childcare, healthcare, every kind of mutual assistance based on kinship, not money. The major factor in the disintegration of modern family life is not "sex" but—listen to the words—"the cost of living." (Not to mention that this nuclear family model is the most ecologically destructive possible; every person their own toilet bowl, washer and drier, refrigerator and computer does create 21st century "individuality," but this Individual as Consumer is swallowing the Earth.) So what was the question?

What is Marriage?

What we all would want, that ideal, "the Marriage of True Minds." The *hieros gamos,* good sex, good conversation, good intention.

Good comprehension, that is, of both Solitude and Union.

This could never be something enforced by Law, although we know that Law historically strives to forbid it. A man who listens to his Woman is not listening to his God, hint, hint.

In *The Masks of God,* Vol. 4, "Creative Mythology," Joseph Campbell describes the invention, in the 12th and 13th century West, of Romantic Love. The groovy Troubadour and Trouvere cultures of southern France, in their leisure and abundance, playing with new toys brought back from the exotic Orient by the Crusaders: Love poetry, incense, hashish, the prototype of the guitar, Erotic Attraction as Art and Game. They were high-class hippies on the edge of The Inquisition; no doubt they provoked the Fires, the revenge of nasty celibate men against lusty Nature (a nastiness echoed in todays religious fundamentalists and political reactionaries, people who went through the 60s as unlaid nerds; who wont rest until Inquisition Redux: Think Ashcroft, think Scalia, think DeLay). Knighthood and Courtly Love are the flowering of this pagan Celtic/Gallic imaginary culture. Because the female was typically married to someone else, she and her lover sought a marriage of true bodies outside the marriage bed; and this remains our literary archetype of the time. But in Chaucer's *Canterbury* Tales, there's a story of a marriage of true minds between two people actually married to each other. It's stunning: "The Franklin's Tale." A man and wife relating by mutual honor and respect, overcoming all via "noble behavior" and "generous magnanimity"—a courageous matrimonial trust that changes the behavior of all around them. Arveragus and his lady, Dorigen, actually make marriage look cool. Notably, this is not a Christian tale; the setting is Armorica, now Brittany in northwest France, a Bretonic Gaelic region.

The couple inherits pagan Celtic tradition, for example, rules of marriage as recorded in the Seancchus Mor, where upper status male and female each brings to the marriage their horse and their sword. A marriage of equals, that is. Marriage lasts one year and one day; at the end of that time, if both desire to remain together, their vows are renewed. If either wants to end the mating, it is ended. Property reverted each to each, what she brought into the marriage she takes with her, and he also. Small children stayed with the mother; in fact they were raised, like all children, by the essential tribe. A mating of true minds can only happen, that is, if each partner is true, and has a mind.

"The Franklin's Tale" is interesting also in that it references pagan or "heathen" science, both astronomy and astrology, climatology and wizardry, oceanography and incantation. Which brings us back round to Question #1: Before and surrounding "Western science" there were other modes of science. Before and surrounding Patriarchal and Biblical marriage, human beings had other ways, just as effective and reasonable in pursuit of social coherence, stable life for children, companionship and guidance through the stages of life and conversation with death.

But here we are now, in the WeirdWiredWest, where each of us is strangely a Clone and an Alien, both at once. Uniform, and estranged. A marriage, in this situation, can be the only sane, humane island in a psychotic sharky sea. The spectacle of True Minds finding and meeting each other, mating and helping each other amidst this Terminal Opera, is rare, but when it happens—and I've known of a few such True Marriages, yrs among them—well, its a beautiful thing.

6
Preferably Knot

Thirteen months of this, let's call it Bartleby]s mix of Pride and Despair. Pride, that is, because "I knew who I was." But who was that, really? A street bum, using taxpayer-funded state intellectual facilities for personal hygiene. If not illegal, shameful. Scum of the earth. Despair, because regardless of what I might have written, or thought, or done, it didnt matter: I was existential Pariah. Books, poetry, radical politics, feminism, a list of self-delusions I carried in my Levi pocket. Nothing matters in America but Money, and we all know that. Who You Are Is Yr Bank Account, Not Yr Mind.

This knowledge, this truth, this fact, is Crushing. The literal weight of it on yr chest stops the heart, pushes air from the lungs. As if the whole megaquadrillion ton weight of Wall St falls on you: But it doesn't even have to fall on you, it crushes virtually, effectively, by just Being There: The Wall of Money. Before which all yr fellow citizens kneel, trembling, in obeisance. If this is America, if this is Reality, then this is Home: Something you have to pay for. Thus Bartleby: The Soul w/out a Home in America.

He is the homeless soul the West has built.

—Barbara Mor

ENGEL: As Melville's Bartleby the Scrivener says, "I would prefer not to." It doesnt really matter, anyway. Not *really*. So, why?

MOR: Street living in Tucson, 1987-88, I'd search out quiet weekend places to do personal hygiene. Washed out shirts, underwear etc., qwik-dri in desert air. The usual public buildings were closed, and the usual BurgerKing, Carls Jr. tiny restrooms—one toilet, one sink—were noisy with weekend families; little boys in womens bathrooms w/their mothers tend to get down on their hands and knees to peek under the stall, its a compulsion to view The Strange Other at Her Worst. And if yr washing yr shorts in the sink, they freak. I chewed raw garlic bulbs to boost my immune system, this created a vampyre-free-zone aura around me that was strategically useful but socially off-putting in close quarters. So I hung out at the U of A [Arizona]; the student center building had a big second floor lounge with rows of sinks and stalls, coolly uninhabited on Sunday mornings. The University, I felt, was sort of "home"—because, well, my book was in the U of A library, it would be used in Womens Studies classes; and hey, I'd applied (unsuccessfully) for work as library clerk, summer press copy editor, and, through the Maintenance Dept., as lounge matron and general toilet bowl cleanser. On Sundays, when others were in Church, it felt luxurious to wash undies and armpits in the big unoccupied second floor lounge, real soap and hot water, a Mental Retreat where homeless American feminist writers might feel "at home" ("misery hides aloof," sez Melville).

Then, one morning, when I was sponge bathing and foot washing, my shirt unbuttoned (no bra, no shoes), the matron suddenly stuck her head around the door, I looked up to see a look of horror on her face, whereupon she turned and ran down the empty hall squealing, "She's bathing in there! She's bathing in there!"

I got out quick, and nothing happened. Except that I never went back. The maid's shock notified me that, of course, UA was not "home" to my body, even though its Library might house my book. The maid didn't see "a writer" but "a public nuisance"—and her perception was, of course, the operative view.

Thirteen months of this, lets call it Bartleby's mix of Pride and Despair. Pride, that is, because "I knew who I was." But who was that, really? A street bum, using taxpayer-funded state intellectual facilities for personal hygiene. If not illegal, shameful. Scum of the earth. Despair, because regardless of what I might have written, or thought, or done, it didnt matter: I was existential Pariah. Books, poetry, radical politics, feminism, a list of self-delusions I carried in my Levi pocket. Nothing matters in America but Money, and we all know that. Who You Are Is Yr Bank Account, Not Yr Mind.

This knowledge, this truth, this fact, is Crushing. The literal weight of it on yr chest stops the heart, pushes air from the lungs. As if the whole megaquadrillion ton weight of Wall St falls on you: But it doesn't even have to fall on you, it crushes virtually, effectively, by just Being There: The Wall of Money. Before which all yr fellow citizens kneel, trembling, in obeisance. If this is America, if this is Reality, then this is Home: Something you have to pay for. Thus Bartleby: The Soul w/out a Home in America.

He is the homeless soul the West has built.

Melville, most American of writers, dreaming Kafka's 20th century in his short stories, in Bartleby creates the Dickensian doppelganger, London's financial, legal and penal architecture transported from Victorian England into 19th-century America (supposedly "a new world")—Wall St, The Tombs, the same gaunt gloomy buildings of biophobic power shutting out light and health, mocking human happiness, rendering work-lives of multitudes—twelve hour days, six days a week—deficient in what landscape painters call "life." And these were the good jobs. No way to catch or grow yr own food. No place to sleep or shit or piss or die or give birth w/out paying the designated fee. The generation and preservation of absolute Law and Wealth, contingent upon the brutal constriction and infliction of the ephemeral Human Being.

The Soul's confrontation w/soulless Machinery: This is America.

A New World for you, Mr. Bartleby.

He'd prefer not. In the Dead Letter office, his previous employment, he'd heard God's answer to mortal hope: Silence. He'd tossed these little prayers into the fire, this was his job. Over the edge of banal despair, he'd looked: There is Nothing. With or without money, that is, the same vision as The American Dream, in the End. It is all illusion, a flatline trying to escape the cosmic Mobius.

Maybe he was born a Zero Man. He's kind of a Zen Legal Secretary. Facing the Wall (which is the word NO), he insisted on his terms. Bartleby knew who he was, unfortunately unbacked by money, but nonetheless. He knew his intrinsic worth, qua human; and he knew he was not wanted unless he rendered this intangible self *usable*—and he preferred not. He took up minimal space or air: Let his sheer existence as Life Datum be honored, allow him to simply sit or stand or sleep in that tiny corner behind his screen, facing his wall—in India, perhaps a Holy Man; in America, a problem of Flesh. A body nonconforming to its designated space. But couldn't the Boss care enough about *him,* in all else impeccable, to allow this? But of course not. No, we all know the Answer: Harrumph harrumph, suppose everyone made such a request? If you allow one, you open the door to everyone. Barbarism! Anarchy! Thus Bartleby threatens to bring the End of Civilization as we know it.

(And, no, I dont want to share my apartment with any of the homeless people who hang out, drinking and bullshitting, on my back porch. I'm tired of cleaning up the cigarette butts and bottles and occasional diarrhea piles they leave behind—I would prefer not!—and when I was homeless I knew such a request was hopeless, also. The "hopelessness of remedying excessive and organic ill.")

Only the Usable are Useful. Despair tells us: Be a Gear, or Die.

An American writer, Joe Napora, sent me some Dickens quotes from G.K. Chesterton's Charles Dickens: *The Last of the Great Men.* On America,

Dickens said: "I do fear that the heaviest blow ever dealt at liberty will be dealt by this country, in the failure of its example on the earth."

On NPR's March 3 *Wait, Wait, Dont Tell Me* quiz show, the host read from a Knight-Ridder news release on that week's reopening of the Statue of Liberty, closed to the Public since 9/11. The monument was described as "a big green woman who invites you to climb to the top of her head, from the earth of her bare feet to her airy brain via a spiral staircase."

Is this not breathtaking? Is this not heartbreaking?

What America was supposed to be. What Life on our Planet was supposed to be. What happened? What have We done to Her, what have They done to Us, what went so unbearably *wrong*?

Bartleby—Melville, of course, who killed the Whale; or Coleridge, who killed the Albatross—deep inside their eyes, the Vision of the Black Hole behind Americas official optimism, our global Boosterism: The Wall of Wealth is built with the bodies of Earth made usable, but then they die, and then they rot. Power rots, and it really stinks. They tell us that stink is the price of our survival.

And some of us will go into the bizness of Perfume.

And some of us will prefer not.

Appendix: An Email Exchange

(Between Eric Larsen, Adam Engel, and Barbara Mor)

LARSEN:

How do these look? Corrections? Improvements? Changes?

ENGEL:

Well, to be honest. . . I think the "general readership" (all fifteen of them), even "our people" (who I wouldn't trust as far as I can throw Oprah Winfrey cause they may be rootin' for us "in theory," but they sure as hell ain't buying, much less reading, our books) need to be led by the nose. Mocked. Humiliated. Forced to face their own fat, ugly faces, smell their fetid junk-food farts, accept the *guilt* of lying on the couch for fifteen, twenty years while the Empire cum Entertainment Center rolls its tanks over men, women, children, animals, flowers and anything displaying even a hint of truth or beauty, anything worth living for and hence—horror of horrors—worth dying for.

I'm cool to put my stuff "out there," and believe Faulkner was right in saying that an artist must at all times be willing to "fall flat on his face," but I'm ultimately far more Lenny Bruce-ian than Faulknerian. I wanna skewer these folks. They deserve, these bloated Americans, these beasts blown from the baloney and cheese-clogged bowels of polyurethane Empire, nothing less than napalm; unfortunately, all I can offer them is

89

piss and vinegar, and even *that's* turning into lemonade and sour grapes.

Give me till Sunday night to come up with my own little homage to the "reading public," this unfathomably insane, inane bevy of thrice-shorn sheeple who empty their wallets for fat, 19th century narratives with 21st century cardboard "characters" and linoleum scenery, yet secretly yearn for the air-headed simplicity and brevity of Bazooka Joe comics and pithy maxims tucked within the sugary folds of tasteless fortune cookies.

I yearn for something far more meaningful than literature: a hearty laugh; a creepy cackle, a not-so-subtly vindictive guffaw. I want to point at their convex bellies and Nixonian jowls and say it loud and clear: "I don't care how much liposuction you paid for this year, YOU'RE FAT!!! God doesn't love you. You're gonna die one day, sooner rather than later, I believe, and disappear into the voidest of voids, FOREVER!!!!! And no one, not even yer mommy and daddy and yer Uncle Sam and yer little dog, two, will give a good goddamn, or even notice, for that matter, that you're gone."

They're sick, depraved, and I'm sick -- of them. They've allowed Big Media to rob us of our literary and intellectual inheritance. We must launch every sentence like a rocket into the hellish ghettos of their cramped little minds. They are like the Germans reflected in the shattered windows of their burning cities, circa 1944—irredeemable. Beyond salvation. Fuck em.

LARSEN:

Youre on! Oliver has plenty of room for this. Onward!

MOR:

I think it's brilliant—the Manifesto[4] is really a
beautiful Manifesto, in its sound as well as
argument. The work in *Cella Fantastik* is also
beautiful & serious, & I assume people will get
this message from Eric's site,
about Adam Engel is brilliant too—except it
blows the camouflage, Belize will begin to have
a booming bizness in people heat-seeking the
trio Morrison/Engel/Rimbaud, & are they ready

---

[4] *Why Bother?: Getting a Life in a Locked-down Land* (Feral House, 2001).

for this? (MorrisonEngel&Rimbaud I mean, I'm
sure Belize is ready—I think it might be necessary
for, e.g., Elvis Costello to appear wearing a longwig
& carrying a butterfly net, to save their TripleAss
TalentBand from being commercially exploited
by those guys who want to contract them for 4
star-turn seasons on Poets of New Oblivion Island,
the cameras never sleep & really like poets with
those holographic eyeballs.
Which Blinks First???

I apologize, I'm just catching up with the dialog on
Cella, have been obsessing on *BR* corrections/etc &
otherwise negotiating dailystuff in & out of long
corridors of rain, hail, & anxiety. Am so looking
forward to the FUN, & the Honor, of these books
coming out, & haunted by the sadistic fear that I &
my computer will disappear in seismic abyss before
it can happen (plus being totally dependent for mere
survival on this govmnt/country/culture that is yes, Adam,
all you note & more—Nietzsche's & Nathaniel West's
Mob of the Terminally Resentful cuz they are FAT
UGLY STUPID & SOMEBODY ISN'T & THEY MUST
PAY—my nerves are old but the sagey luster is wearing thin.
That being said: Nothing Eric wrote in his Cella blurb
is 'over the top'—it's a magnificent serious work; those
who know the ranter/joker will be required to respect
this work at a depthier level than they expect going into
its pages. The entire enterprise of 'selling'—books, gods,
oneself, everything—is so saturated, we can't believe our
own words when we talk 'about' our own work. I don't
believe it's possible any more to really 'talk about' a
work of writing without distortion, or shortchange, or
hyped diversion. In fact, just silently hand someone a
book, tell them to read it first & THEN any discourse
begins—about, for, or against it. Nothing else is pure.
So, Eric's first venture doesn't seem overblown to
me, on the contrary, very respectful. But definitely
it's yr writing, meaning: you know the (imagined/
real) reader you want to talk to.
When it comes to a Press, to Get Attention for
outrageous promo words (yr words, in this case)
is ALSO an act of Hype: the test is the same: Does
the Actual Work back it up in Power, Originality &

Sheer Skilled Guts, or Not? I think *Cella* is strong
enough to endure any test of promo rave or rant,
so my opinion is rather mild or neutral (a Libra): I
trust the WORK to do the work of promotion, the
issue is to get it to the attention of those who still
are able to attend. And who are they? It's a relay
race at this point: who can catch the books & help
carry them forward? Cuz I don't know; promo is
expected from a Press, & I think *in any form* you
choose, it has to be accepted for what it is. Who
are we talking to now—Oliver has the blithe free
opportunity to MAKE a reputation, not burdened
with just maintaining or pandering a market. That is,
it's DIY. And then—who, what is it handed over to
next? I have no names of reviewers trustable to really
read a book, except maybe—Curtis White, who already
knows yr work. My ideal readers at this point are
Greil Marcus & Howard Hampton, music & film critics/
reviewers; & totally out of my reach. Once they would
be there in *Village Voice,* gone now. *BookForum* I do
read, but they aren't necessarily geniuses—one or two
of their reviewers might be for Cella, a lot of them would be
McSweeneyEggarsFoster wannabes or Oates/Oliver/Picoult
girlgroupies who don't want to hear what you're telling them
—it's all a crapshoot once the book enters the world. I
don't have any ideas for negotiating this world—do you?
Sorry I'm so lame, but I am.
Barbara

ENGEL:

Those names, Morrison & Rimbaud, bring to mind those folks who arrive at a place, define or help define a "scene," and by the time the herd and their retailers "get it" the originators are bored stiff, causing them to A: die young: Fitzgerald, Kerouac, Acker and, for that matter, Morrison and Rimbaud themselves; B: retreat ever deeper into the proverbial "studio" to pursue their art to its limits and then suddenly stop, at least publicly: again Rimbaud, Garbo, Salinger, The Beatles; C: stop for a while, then for god knows what reason (money? ego? loneliness?) come back as a poor imitation of their best selves until even former advocates (comme moi) turn away in disgust: Elvis, Pynchon, Dylan, The Rolling Stones.

But there is that certain rare artist who, unlike Yeats, Stein, Wallace Stevens, WCW, and my "fellow Brooklynite," Marianne Moore, create a quick burst of masterpieces that really constitute one "Monsterpiece" (usually within the span of a single decade) that explodes upon the culture, influencing the way a generation thinks, acts, dresses, and even speaks: Fitzgerald, Hemingway, Dylan Thomas, Salinger, Mailer, The Beats, Pynchon, Patti Smith and her then "boyfriend," Sam Shepherd (who, like Pynchon, had to cross the continent to find his True (West) Voice). Unfortunately, the immense energy required of these people literally burns them out within a decade of intense production, either killing them outright (Acker), causing them to kill themselves via booze and drugs (Fitzgerald, Hemingway, Corso, Kerouac, Morrison, Janis Joplin, Jimi Hendrix, etc.), or to go crazy—possibly from desire to "recapture the magic"? be relevent again? or is it simply that they run out of money and don't know how to do anything else? Pynchon, Mailer, The Stones, Dylan, Ginsberg, Elvis, Judy Garland, and god knows how many others—let's not forget Sinatra—murder their own best selves this way.

Rare are the wise ones—Salinger, the Beatles, Shepherd, Patti Smith, Garbo, and a few others—who know that when it's time to sit down and shut the fuck up (at least publicly) actually do sit down and shut the fuck up (perhaps this explains the popularity, among such people, of yoga, Zen, Taoism and other eastern philosophy/religions whose basic tenets are, more or less: sit down and shut the fuck up!).

Even more rare are the Monster Geniuses who continue to produce great work upon great work till wise old age (even, like Yeats, Stevens, and my old thesis advisor, Allen Grossman, getting better, or at least reaching "the palm at the end of the mind" that is the logical consequence of their life's work): Mumford, Stein, Mann, Marianne Moore. . .

It ain't easy, this "civilized life." I totally agree with Jensen (and Keats, though he wasn't aware of what he was doing in this regard): stop "evolving" at the stone-age point, live in small tribes or communities in which everyone is at least an acquaintance—250 people at most, according to research, or "compassion fatigue" sets in and you could give a goddamn about the strangers you drop nuclear weapons on—in which art, spirituality, craft, language, both for pleasure and instruction (poetry) and communication, are all integrated into one's day-to-day existence. The only real changes needed were the only ones that mattered and still matter, especially since humans have, if anything, devolved morally, emotionally and spiritually, at roughly the same pace their masters have evolved tech-illogically: staring at the Abyss and learning not to flinch when the Abyss stares back; re-integrating the male and female at both the socio-economic level as well as the moral, behavioral, spiritual, into ONE race rather than two separate but unequal "partners" in procreation and maintenance of the "procreated" through the 20 or so years necessary—even in tribal cultures—to learn how to become "human."

MOR:

Eric & Adam,
I've sent in mail a copy of Powell's requirements for getting them to carry books; it's called Dear Author....
uh huh.
I haven't been able to breach their 'firewall' to talk to Gerry Daneghy or anyone else involved in accepting new books/presses into their store. Twice I took all the books downtown & asked to see Daneghy or make an appointment; 2 different women at mainfloor Info Desk (Lit, both regular & smallpress, is located on the mainfloor all around them) told me that Powell's gets a whole cart of newly submitted books every day, & so they've changed their policies to deal w/the flood. Both were very nice; I told them none of us were amateurs: have published both in print & online, books I'm carrying (Topiary, Cella, Yorick & BR) are online at Amazon, Barnes&Noble & other websites; I have a HarperCollins book that's been on their Women's Mythology shelves probably since 1990 & used in women's studies classes at PSU etc (I didn't utter the book's *Name*).[5] But no go.
Their requirements include sending nonreturnable copy of book to Powell's; author's name &/or press details etc; obvious stuff. Plus: books' summary or description; name of distributors who carry book(s) if applicable (having what they call a 'major distributor' makes it easier for them); plus shipping information, return policy & discount info if the book is orderable only thru specific author or smallpress. Finally, they won't deal with emails or websites; you must send them via mail all this info:
Powell's Books
Purchasing Dept.
2720 NW 29th Avenue
Portland, OR 97210

---

[5] *The Great Cosmic Mother: Rediscovering the Religion of the Earth* (Harper & Row, 1987). The book's title was not Mor's choice. Her original title had been The First God.

Very depressing to me; I figured being a local would give me some access. And again, I personally (visually) am not an impressive character unless the subject is admission into an oldage ward.

Has there been any response/contact with Drew Swenhaugen at Hawthorne Powell's? Ditto: with Small Press Distribution in Berkeley? AK Press/Distribution in Oakland? or (remote possibility) AK Distribution in Edinburgh?
If so, I would want to inform Powell's of this; they give Ingram, Bker&Taylor, KoenPacific & Bookpeople as examples of 'major distributors' but I know SPD has been around a long time as small/indy press distributors, & they're right down the fucking coast.
(May or may not be relevant: Powell's just laid off lots of its workers, lots of disgruntlement as everywhere & no doubt they are all overworked due to this. As the flood of self-published endtimes memoirs pours in daily....BUT The Oliver shouldn't be in this sad category, it has put out books for 2+ years with a functioning website, writers who are not publishing for the first time but have some reputation in their fields, etc. So these are all lumped in together, mass entertainingly, with Aunt Betsy getting her family reminiscences & favorite recipes into print before she & all these Sludge Idaho memories die forever???)
Well, onward: I'm sending in a BR copy to their address with required info; & you can do same from your end. Any working relationship with a book distributor, major or at least WestCoast, would definitely help. I guess online from Amazon, B&N, doesn't count??? At one point, I saw BlueRental on Powell's online list, but now I can't find it....a rose is not a rose it's an Industry.

LARSEN:

Time has stretched out, or gotten compressed, or some damn thing, whatever causes it to be in shorter and shorter and shorter supply. Something has happened to it, that's for sure. Apologies for my out-of-touchness.

Damn Powell's, damn all the Bigs. You know, Barbara, the damnedest thing is that Oliver books ARE distributed by Ingram. Lightning Source, the printer, is a company created by the Ingram family for the very purpose of making/allowing print-on-demand books be part of their/its distributional kingdom. All of our books can be ordered by any bookstore in the US, Canada, England, and the EU--plus, as soon as I can find time (troubled concept, that fucking time) to fill out the proper forms (have already gotten 'em), Australia, a place where as I understand it people actually do go into bookstores.

So. What does this mean? Nothin', I suspect, to the likes of Powell's. Still, I'm awed by your efforts, Barbara, and by your human armor, at pitting yourself up against the Powell's armored wall. Did it myself when last in Portland and had much the same experience as you describe, except that I did get a name--who?--to call, and did call, and did get that person's agreement to receive our emails, newletters, etc. Does that mean anything? Doesn't seem so.

Even so, I'm willing to pack up each of our ten books separately and mail 'em out to Portland/Powells with the requisite info as reported by you. Why not? Better than having you wear yourself out yet more and yet again. Well, maybe not all ten, but the most recent three or somewhat more.

Poetry! Got four more volumes coming after Yorick. Then many other riches.

Damn, damn, damn, damn. I sent books and requisite info to the small press dist. in Berkeley. No word back. But am afraid that I failed to follow through with the Oakland or Edinburgh ones. I can still search email, find the info from you, and do it. Damn, damn, damn, damn, am wondering though what good in the effort there might be. . . . Advice?

What's wrong with me I don't know for sure. Something massive, I'm sure. These damned articles among the culprits. And yet, shouldn't they generate some Oliver interest? Damned if they seem to.

Wise man wd. quit now? Maybe.

MOR:

Eric & Adam,
I think the article/review of Paul Craig Roberts is important in the general movement of things...lots of stuff needs to be moved along together! both radical politics & radical lit.
Most personally, I don't/can't get focussed or even hung up on the *How* of 9/11; however it happened, I know it happened by intent, & this is the BigMeme that needs to be constantly pushed.

Right now, the undermining (probably not total collapse) of Rupert Murdoch's tumorous brain grip & extension into the bowels of the world. How such a massive *conspiratorial empire* can exist, be sustained, over a long public time with everyone knowing, in their gut instinct, that it is massively corrupt, this is a process now played before our eyes -- nothing new about it, read Western history; but each generation thinks that history is *Past History,* & smugly assumes *it can't happen here.* Or again. duh. Australia, UK & US rotten w/Murdoch, yet his power grew unquestioned; the hierarchy-of-males-in power scenario (& females ditto, so long as they/we seek careers/positions, professions within that system we/they must become its players & reinforcers: reformist politics where people Ask Permission to Enter the Machine just forgets/denies that in that process the Machine Enters You) -- where ambition of the young to get into great celebrity vocations, of the older to maintain their jobs, plus the terror of what happens to whistleblowers or critics of any kind (You're Not One of Us, not only are you Fired, you're DEAD) – reveals how a machinery *everybody knows is rotten* is maintained. Yes, as Adam sez, it's US, stupids; between The Fear & The Career, we keep it going, & the evil ones (Murdoch, Ailes, Goebbels, etc) know that once the Machinery of Coercive Power (coercion by Money &/or Threat of Force) is established (FOXNews in US ran for years in the red, Murdoch absorbed the losses just waiting for the poison to spread sufficiently to addict the critical number of listeners/viewers, & then the EvilWheel turns on its own, voila!).

On such massive scale, the EvilIdol historically isn't ever overturned or destroyed by 'good people' or by revolution from 'without.' It has to self-destruct; as MurdochUK is doing now: all the Brit politicos, right to left, are Shocked! Shocked! Outraged! Outraged! by revelations that News of the World etc etc hack email, blackmail, bribe & ultimately strongarm w/threat of annihilation any rebuttal to their power; only when the Machine gets so fed on its own poison (hubris: absolute power = absolute psychosis), does it then make one further step, overreaches, & falls into its self-created chasm (or whatever metaphor of Implosion works best!). Step too far: hacking into email of child abducted, raped & murdered, thus impeding investigation

& brainfucking her parents -- that is pretty ugly. The Brutal finally provokes the Sentimental (somebody's apt description of German Fascism (Thomas Wolfe?) depicted the enabling German traits as Sentimentality/Brutality) & DerFolk begin to leave their cheering&blubbering on the couch before the BroadcastScreen & barge out in mobs to castrate the Head of the BroadcastSystem. What does it take to make that happen here, US? I saw Oliver stone's JFK first time last week on local tvmovie station; pretty good at depicting the requisite network of petty careerists & grubby exigencies that glue the web together & sustain a complex project w/out anyone really knowing the whole plot or other players in it. It works rhizomically; a process/pattern we don't study here (Americans barely cognize a 4th Dimension let alone those gnarly French theoretical Deleuzean[6] growths!). So it just spreads itself, Power & Secrecy tumoring out in all dimensions as one process. Thus Murdoch's Empire; the entire Set of Game Equations America has been working on/worked by since JFK's death certainly; which itself was set in place/motion by the creepy crossdressing tentacles of JEdgarHoover's FBI over politicians/criminal organizations/police systems. Hey: Santa Claus is a Dirty Old Man -- deal w/it!!!! And his Wife is a drunk or pill addict just to walk out the door into the cameras (pace BettyFord), or freaks out & gets drug into the crazyhotel (John Mitchell's wife, Margaret?) or...she turns into stone & moves to Greece (JackieO), cuz the Kennedys knew it wasn't just LoneAssassin, but shit: how many of *them* have to die? Answer: a few more, one way or another; killed by Power, or self-destructed by Secrecy. I also don't think ThePeople'sDemand toKnow is provoked by insider/esoteric data, however significant (how exactly did WTC collapse/implode/disintegrate, etc) but only by something equivalently Tabloid in its gross & mass-sentiment-revolting proportions: e.g. they hacked emails of Brit soldiers killed in Iraq & Afghanistan, OUR LADS DESECRATED!!! They hacked emails of 9/11 families...Murdoch the TRAITOR!!!! PARASITE ON WESTERN CIVILIZATION!!!! SERIAL RAPIST &

---

[6] Reference to Gilles Delouze, philosopher and writer (1925–1995).

MUTILATOR OF THE MOTHER TONGUE!!!!!
Well...I won't hold any breath waiting for US Media to turn totally on FOX/WallStreetJournal/TVGUIDE/ HARPERCOLLINS (teehee)...cuz they all in the same snakepit. But, short of this OverwhelmingMassUrge to Decapitate the Tyrant (which periodically does emerge & do its thing), the only effective rebuttal is to work the general message, in Art/Avant projects, in writing, over & over, This Ain't Denmark, Kiddoes, But Something Is Rotten— It Must Be Yrs. The Young will proceed from there, take it from there; I don't think the LeftEnlightened doing its usual circle-shooting on particular Details, the group-suicide spectacles of Expertise-in-Debate w/Itself, is *dismissable* at this point-- but it's a habit of the Intellect that has proved a distraction from the general dynamics of empowering a Movement of Rage/Outrage that can get the job done: provoke the Mass to WakeUp&Fight for their lives against 1)Power & 2)theFearSystem that fuels/maintains it. Broad categories; i.e. massive armies of generalized message. Not what intellectuals usually do; or serious artists. We set the basic memes in motion, however -- ergo, important to avoid dismissal into categories of 'crackpot theories' etc. which Power's *mediaworks* have in place just for this dandy disposal purpose.
As for time, it's never enough.
Barbara

ENGEL:

Rupert Murdoch, scrofulous scion of a "proletariat" too lumpen to make it as extras in a 900 page Dickens novel. Don't get me wrong, I'm no Dickens-basher (in *Hard Times* he "*mot-juste*-ed" almost on a level with Turgenev and Flaubert), but the guy got paid by the word, and these lumps-of-prole *still* wound up on the cutting-room floor. What was poor Albion to do but soak 'em in gin and cheap-assed rum till they were literally flammable and toss 'em like Molotov cocktails at the aborigines of Australia? But Rupert made something of himself: a Royal (nod to "mother England?") international pain-in-the-ass. "Publisher" of the *NY Post, Harping Collards* books, et al.

LARSEN:

Barbara, Adam,

Am wondering whether it all is "dismissable," things having gone as far as they have. What I wonder is whether any "waking up" can, will occur, or is any longer capable of occurring.

Past two a.m. now, must fall into arms of Morpheus. But. I'm very much wondering yet again whether many of these extraordinary letters can't be and shouldn't be gathered and brought into print. PDQ. Time is short--as in "never enough."

ENGEL:

And for everyone's after-hours entertainment, let us now dance to the Hurdy-Gurdy, an instrument most appropriate for "our time." If one recalls, one of the most popular "early" video games from the 80s was "Mario Brothers" featuring Hurdy-Gurdy type "paesans" and a monkey (or several); Lanier's subtle and deeply ironic.[7] He literally saw the horrible fruits of his creation and opted out. As if Victor Frankenstein escaped from Antarctica and his ugly, resentful "son," and set up a chess table in the park, charging/wagering a dollar per game...

But ultimately it becomes a question of, in the "field" of the written word, a year's subscription to TIME Magazine/the NY Times, i.e. just a whole lotta never-to-be-read words that, even if read, will be long forgotten by Monday's first Latte -- or a Fortune Cookie that explodes in yer face and shatters your most cherished beliefs and breaks your heart. David and his single-stone stoving in Goliath's fat head like a balsa-wood whale boat speared by Moby Dick, sending the Philistines the volk the masses the slaves the herd scattering...

Forget about the "form" and "aesthetics" I've been pounding my head against the wall for 30 years to try to convey: Keatsian beauty; Kafkaesque horror and hysteria; Pynchon/David Lynch atmosphere of the violent androgyny and paranoia beyond the illusions of white-picket-fence "normalcy." These things I've tried to reach for in my "work," particularly Topiary and Cella.

Fuck it all. Fuck it to death. Fuck it till it pukes blood and clump-chunks of clotted jissom...

These times demand pith and mockery. Aphorisms. Stuff you can fire

---

[7] Jaron Lanier, author of *You Are Not a Gadget* (Knopf, 2010), etc.

point-black into the page or explode like a grenade at Thanksgiving Dinner....

Nietzsche; LaRoachFooledCold; Twain, Oscar Wilde, Ambrose Bierce. Crotchety old Mencken. Nasty Dorothy Parker with a dash of Gilda Ratner. Chris Rock, Richard Pryor Lenny Bruce. Phyllis Diller. Lou Reed and Laurie Anderson for post-modern irony and a celebration of union, sexual, intellectual and otherwise, of REAL artists...

Or as Stevens wrote, in some poem,[8] I forgot which: "The mockers. The mickey mockers!"

Wit-tle them away.

MOR:

Yes, allthese DeepThoughts ARE important, if only we could believe they would be read by anybody else....In regard to the never dismissable details: they are *sine qua non* Evidence in a Court of Law, i.e. absolutely critical. My mood just comes from decades (we've all witnessed) watching TheBestMinds of theLeft deploy major energy dissecting & demoralizing EachOther while less finely-tuned Armies of theStupid stomp over us, planet & Future. This General in-house arena of BrainDisplay (easier to trash others powerless like us rather than storm WallSt Exxon FBI Pentagon etc) enervated Feminism more than any other single factor; the mutual carpal blogging of Lefter-Than-Thou factions is an Industry etc; & this is human & human ain't dismissable. My usually grim mood is just that a GeneralConsensus must be maintained against the usual factioning into quarreling lone brilliant authors-- cuz it's a solid wall of psychotic Money & Panic out there: Rove Ailes et al will KILL (already have) to maintain Power cuz they know -- more than anybody -- this is the only way to keep their asses out of prison for Life. Singleminded motivation: w/all the Money & all the Guns, real scary! When it comes to conspiracy theories, e.g., ThomHartmann has co-authored a 2000 page kind of evidenciary trove on

---

[8] "American Sublime"

JFK's assassination, worked on for decades; conclusion:
Mafia & Cubans mostly; Hartmann is a brilliant prolific
guy, but doubts Pentagon, Hoover's FBI, Dallas police
were involved (southern racism of course involved, as in
MLK's shooting). Oliver Stone sees what I see: Hoover
up to his eyeballs w/Pentagon faction collusion *of course*.
If Cubans, only becuz they were criminal types; the
Mafiaorganized crime also, which always colluded
w/Hoover in maintaining their mutual biz status quo.
Anyway: all I know is that 1) widespread plots of
assassination, including 9/11, ARE capable of not
only execution but successful 'coverup' for years,
decades, on a global 24/7 screen -- not because folks
don't *see/sens*e it, but that seeing & sensing such
RulingRot is so frightening most people reach for the
Wipe-Out White-Out whatever....change the channel,
open the booze, watch FOXnews....the 2000 election,
everybody knows it was a *coup,* a criminal coup. We
choose to live w/it; the stress of Otherwise is too
much. So today the major witness against a collusion
of UK Cameron with Murdoch -- Sean Hoare,who
worked for News of the World -- was found dead in
his home; coinkidinky? Brit Police say nothing looks
suspicious. Nobody told them to say this, right? Cuz
of course all the head cops are involved too...process
banal by now in its description, but I don't think The
Left gives enough serious thought to what happens
when mass self-medication DOES wake up & smell the
corpses -- uh, are we all assumed to have passports
& guaranteed employment elsewhere? (e.g. Cockburn,
Ted Rall, et al). What I saw in the 60s, playing with
Revolution, a lot of black guys died, young white women
also (SLA house conflagration in LA, another in Philly,
others other places)...martyrs to a Revolution that just
never happened: LeftMinds went on to academic jobs,
everybody just calm down! And everything I walked
out of 6 years of (unpaid debt) college for – FemaleBrain
Revolution! yeah! -- just dissolved, into sororities of
IdentityPolitics & disappearance of bookstores, the
concept of StrongMindedWomen just grotesquely
absorbed into Oprah, gourmet cooking, Mama Grizzlies
& chicklit. Okay, the World Turns, thats a soap opera.
Rightwing Tyrannies establish churches, banks, media
empires, think tanks, armies. LeftRevolutions become

Soap Operas ??!! They always seem to have the money & power & institutional structure to just wait things out while we do this to ourselves....including my rant, over & over, outloud to my cat or via email.
I think establishing a Press is a real move to build a real thing that can stand its ground in such a flood of crazy energies, & I'm very grateful you have done it. The discouragement of not finding readers, is this just another way of saying We are American writers? Or maybe we're just impatient. I truly don't know. I now hope that Eckhard Puehse, when he gets the book, will send some feedback to Oliver (yr return address on it), even if he howls in buyer's remorse it will be a REAL LIVE RESPONSE, what fun. In fact, I envy anyone who has access to a hurdygurdy & can play it -- very difficult instrument, very expensive. They are very wonderful, the only sound to make in reply to the world.

End of Conversation

A NOTE:
BARBARA MOR
ON WRITING SERIOUSLY TODAY

BookForum (Apr/May 2009, pg 48) reported on an April 14 panel held at The New York Public Library titled "The Death of Boom Culture":

Now that markets have proved a flawed index of our economic well-being, our cultural life needs to look beyond the pat certainties of laissez-faire ideology. Among the ills afflicting the American novel at the height of boom culture, Walter Benn Michaels argues, was a curatorial obsession with past oppressions—from slavery to the Holocaust to family abuse, recounted memoir-style. Writers should now be asking less about what it meant to endure the Holocaust, he contends, and more about what it means to support free trade.

Barbara Mor agrees:

Our planet is a theater of sublime cannibalism—our lives have always been sustained by the deaths of other living things, & vice versa: it's an organic recycling process that, within the self-regulations & conservations of Nature, works. As a run-amok global factory & marketing system based on a corporate cannibalism that is regulated solely by the sharky appetites of Capital, Earth becomes a Factory of Horror. Writers respond to this by curling inward around personal pain, or reaching backward to connect with the larger agonies of human-made past history.

But the Enormous Poem, in such a world, exists *now & everywhere*. It is *inside us & there,* performing sleeplessly 24/7: tragic epic, colossally cruelly funny drama, deadpan news items from hell. No extant "literary convention" approaches it. The writer/poet must see it for what it is without euphemistic self-protection; look long & hard without blinking or descent into memoirist babbling—& it will pour molten into yr eyes & brain forever.

And then, with yr eyeballs burnt out & yr tongue charbroiled, you proceed to (try to) write. Play yr sacrificial part in this terrible feast. All the repressed gods &/or monsters from all the repressed mythologies ever on earth are now returning to join you.

ALSO AVAILABLE FROM
THE OLIVER ARTS & OPEN PRESS

FICTION

THE DECLINE AND FALL OF THE AMERICAN NATION, Novel by Eric Larsen (2013)

THE END OF THE 19TH CENTURY, Novel by Eric Larsen (2012)

THE BLUE RENTAL, Texts by Barbara Mor, (2011)

ABLONG, Novel by Alan Salant (2010)

KIMCHEE DAYS, Novel by Timothy Gatto (2010)

TOPIARY, A Modular Novel by Adam Engel (2009)

NONFICTION

DANCE WITHOUT STEPS, Memoir by Paul Bendix (2012)

THE SKULL OF YORICK, Essays on the Cover-up of 9/11 by Eric Larsen (2011)

AFGHANISTAN: A WINDOW ON THE TRAGEDY, by Alen Silva (2011)

I HOPE MY CORPSE GIVES YOU THE PLAGUE, Essays by Adam Engel (2010)

HOMER FOR REAL: A READING OF THE ILIAD by Eric Larsen (2009)

FROM COMPLICITY TO CONTEMPT, Essays by Timothy Gatto (2009)

POETRY

A CROW'S DREAM, Poetry by Douglas Valentine (2012)

THE BOOK OF TRANSPARENCIES, Poetry by Gregory Marszal (2012)

LISTENING TO THE THUNDER, Poems by Helen Tzagoloff (2012)

THE EXPEDITION SETS OUT, Poetry by Alan Salant (2011)

AUTUMN LAMP IN RAIN, Poetry by Han Glassman (2011)

CELLA FANTASTIK, Prose Cartoons by Adam Engel (2011)

I AM NOT DEAD, Poetry by Gregory Marszal (2010)

Oliver titles are available through any bookseller or at
www.oliveropenpress.com

We hope *the Victory of sex & Metal* inspires you to look at other Oliver titles.

How did you hear about us? Would you recommend this and/or other Oliver titles to a friend?

Did you purchase this title online, from one of the "usual online dealers," or from the Oliver website?

Did you find this title in a local bookstore?

Please contact us about this book and other Oliver titles you might have read.

Email Oliver's editor and publisher, Eric Larsen:
editor@oliveropenpress.com
or Oliver's associate editor, Adam Engel:
assoceditor@oliveropenpress.com

You can also reach the press by mail:
The Oliver Arts & Open Press
2578 Broadway, Suite #102
New York, New York 10025

Colophon

———

As requested by Barbara Mor, this book is designed in Times Roman. Mor composed her work in ten-point Roman and insisted there be no change in appearance between typescript and printed page.

www.ingramcontent.com/pod-product-compliance
Lightning Source LLC
LaVergne TN
LVHW051645080426
835511LV00016B/2506